RETIREMENT 'KNOW-IT-ALL'™

*'How you look at your money
is very different than
how others do!'*

BY
JOSEPH THOMAS

ISBN 978-1-4951-3944-4

Published by:
Retirement Network Services, Inc.
P.O. Box 2507 | Jupiter, FL 33468
800.227.0595

BACKGROUND: JOSEPH THOMAS

Born in 1960 on a Marine Corps base in Quantico, Virginia, I was on the move most of my early life as a so-called "Marine brat." My father retired from the Marines. However, he still kept moving from the East to West Coasts, so I guess traveling was in his blood. I learned many things quickly, and I was educated on the road while attending many schools. I enjoyed traveling, and I thank my parents for raising our family on the road. Looking back, they did a great job raising the family, even through challenges.

I graduated from high school in San Clemente, California, in 1978 and attended college in New York. I studied at CW Post Long Island University and majored in marketing and management, earning a bachelor of science in business.

In 1981, I married my wife, Lynn, and moved to New Jersey, where I went to work for **John Hancock.** I answered an ad for a marketing representative and took the job not knowing I would start my career in the insurance business. I enjoyed what I was doing for 14 years, and I became a star agent, earning Hancock's highest awards, such as Honor Club and President's Club, numerous times.

I am most proud that I became a five-time qualifying member of the **Million Dollar Round Table.** I truly believe the beliefs instilled by this prestigious and ethical organization shaped my career.

MILLION DOLLAR
ROUND TABLE DISTINCTION

"If your life insurance agent or financial services advisor is a member of MDRT, be assured that you are working with an accomplished, ethical professional who is considered to be among the best in the world. Round Table membership is an exclusive honor that is achieved only by a small percentage of all life insurance and financial services advisors nationwide." Attaining membership in MDRT is a distinguishing career milestone achieved by less than one percent of the world's life insurance and financial service professionals.

By the end of my career at John Hancock, I had become a financial planner and kept studying and learning as much as possible about the financial business.

In 1994, I moved to North Carolina for a job with **First Union Bank** in a new position called financial consultant. My job included all areas of the bank for new and existing clients, and I worked in the **private client group,** which handled high net worth individuals.

Helping these clients with their money issues taught me many things about how they valued information and used that information to make good business decisions.

The private client group was devoted to reducing taxes while increasing net worth. I found I had a passion for helping clients with protecting their assets, reducing taxes, and making more money for them than they already had accumulated. My career was starting to shape itself into what I wanted to accomplish for myself and my clients. I mastered many valuable aspects of the banking business and developed a very good understanding of how the insurance and banking businesses could work together.

At this point, a very wealthy client (who used to make tanks for the government) in Jupiter, Florida, asked me to come to Florida to review his seven-figure IRA. He asked that I manage it for him, on one condition — that I come to Jupiter once a year to review his account. As a result, I went to Jupiter annually.

I decided to move to Jupiter full-time in 2001, and I learned why it was such a popular place with families and also with the wealthy, who call this area home (or home away from home). Their ranks include Burt Reynolds, Tiger Woods, Michael Jordan, Greg Norman, Gary Player and Celine Dion, among others. Some of the wealthiest people in the world are residents of Jupiter, Jupiter Island, Palm Beach and Palm Beach County. Some say it is because of its beauty. Others say it is because of the Florida weather. I believe it is because wealthy people always know where other wealthy people live.

Florida also has tax laws that work in favor of the wealthy, such as favorable homestead laws and a lack of state income taxes. In addition, Florida happens to be one of the most beautiful states in the country (as I can attest after living all over the United States).

Shortly after moving to Jupiter, I decided to put my insurance and banking skills to work for new clients. I started my own financial service business, called **Retirement Network Services.**

My goal was to offer clients all the financial products needed for a sound retirement by specializing in financial, estate and retirement planning while emphasizing a proactive way to reduce or eliminate taxes during and after retirement. **It is my belief that every person, no matter what level of wealth, should prepare for and protect their assets in every way possible.** My first priority is helping people protect their retirement money and reach their individual goals.

My goal to educate myself continued throughout my career, and as a result, I have been studying all aspects of the financial and retirement business since 1981. My research continues through reading books, attending classes, expos, and seminars, and by completing continuing education courses for my licensing requirements. I take part in seminars hosted by some of the world's leading retirement and tax experts so that I can maintain and keep up with the ever-changing financial world.

In 2005, I was asked to speak on a radio show in South Florida about how I help people who are retired or planning for retirement. I enjoyed the feeling of being on the air and giving people advice, and I received many compliments from doing the show. I was encouraged to shortly afterward start my own radio show, called *The Retirement Show with Joe Thomas.*

My radio show is broadcast on three AM and FM stations — WBZT, WJNO and WJTW in Florida — and topics include taxes, insurance, retirement and estate planning. I also include investment advice and how to protect your money from the Bernie Madoffs of the world. I discuss how people should protect and educate themselves in making tough decisions before and after retirement. I found that most of my competition was selling products rather than educating clients. Because I offer education, listeners respond very well to my format.

I am writing this book to help people and to pass along the knowledge that I have accumulated after being in the financial world for over thirty years.

This book, *The Retirement "Know-It-All,"* is an overview of what people of any age or wealth status should know when planning for or investing for their retirement. It also outlines the mistakes you need to avoid and, most importantly, a plan of action you need to establish before you make costly mistakes that can affect your bottom dollar throughout your retirement.

The book is also about choosing the right advisor and the right investment choices for the specific problems at hand, and how this can make a huge difference in your financial well-being. Every advisor should have the heart of a teacher. If yours does not, use someone else.

The most important lesson about retirement is that it is crucial to educate yourself before making any financial decisions. This is never more true than in talking about retirement. Because retirement planning can be such a complicated area of expertise, many advisors are simply giving the wrong advice today. Getting a second opinion can be very valuable to make sure you are on the right track in the complicated financial world.

I have always believed in self-education and mastering my craft. This is the reason behind writing this book so that every retiree can learn some of the most important basics needed to know and understand when choosing a retirement plan or talking with a financial advisor. There are many complicated choices for you to make over the course of your retirement lifetime, and you must be and stay informed.

I hope you enjoy the book.

PREFACE

I would like to start by explaining what is meant by the title of this book, *The Retirement "Know-It-All,"* because it is a little bit of a tongue-in-cheek title. It is quite impossible for anyone to know all the nuances of retirement planning in its entirety. Yet many people today, including advisors, think they do know it all, and this can mean devastating results for the uneducated investor or retiree. Hopefully, after reading this book, you will be able to understand the basics of protecting yourself and your money from the know-it-alls of the financial world.

In today's world, there are so many conflicting and differing financial opinions given that, unfortunately, it is up to the investor which of these opinions he or she should choose. Research and self-education is vitally important for the average investor. It is more so today than ever before, because you can lose your money much faster than in years past with the advent of technology, the Internet and high-speed communication. Therefore, it is imperative to become somewhat of a know-it-all for your own protection when it comes to your money and investing for your retirement. I have found that a retiree's success rate can be significantly increased simply by understanding the basics.

If being in the financial world over the past 30 years has taught me one thing, it is that so many retirees are obtaining their recommendations from the wrong advisors, both personally and professionally. Many retirees are taking recommendations not only from uninformed or biased licensed advisors but also from others who may not be an expert or have any necessary knowledge about investing at all. These people are the know-it-alls who can hurt your assets if you are not careful.

Knowledge and expertise in the retirement arena is something I needed if I was going to establish myself as an expert in the world of money and finance. Therefore, I learned as much as I could, so that I could make educated recommendations to my clients without a biased opinion.

Today, many retirees are accepting advice from friends, relatives and the "wrong advisors" for their specific retirement planning goals. This is not a good thing. Reading this book will help you open your eyes to how you should look at your retirement plans — and at those people helping with that advice.

My goal for writing this book is to simply provide you with the information, education and tricks of the trade that I have accumulated in retirement planning. Thus, you can educate yourself, choose the right advisor, reduce costs associated with investing, avoid mistakes others make, learn how to choose your retirement plan, put that plan into action, and decide what type of investor you may be.

Each one of these ideas or concepts in the book may make a big difference in your retirement plans, and they all add up to make huge differences over a lifetime of investing for those who take advantage and implement some basics in their retirement lives.

Again, I hope you enjoy the book.

THE RETIREMENT 'KNOW-IT-ALL'

'How you look at your money is very different than how others do!'

CONTENTS

1. Education 1

2. Advisors 17

3. Costs 37

4. Mistakes 51

5. Plans 73

6. Plan of Action 93

7. Investor Types 105

1
EDUCATION

Education: *the act or process of imparting or acquiring general knowledge, developing the powers of reasoning and judgment, and generally preparing oneself or others intellectually for mature life.*

Robert Kiyosaki, the author of "Rich Dad, Poor Dad" said: "The better your investment education, the better investment advice you will receive."

In today's complex world of finance, it is virtually impossible for a person to "know it all" when it comes to retirement; especially when it comes to choosing an advisor or the financial products they offer. Too little knowledge can be a dangerous thing. Therefore, the most important prerequisite for an investor thinking about or planning for retirement should be to first educate themselves.

It is vital to learn as much as possible before choosing your retirement or investment plan and the products or services offered by the financial advisor. Serious investors need textbooks and education more than they need ideas or predictions from their advisors.

<u>**Please know that there are no magic bullets, no magic pills, no shortcuts and certainly no secrets to retirement planning.**</u> There is only hard work and self-education — learning as much as you can about your money so you do not make mistakes that can cost you your life savings literally.

Retirement, for the purpose of this book, means pre- and post-retirement planning, so whether you are planning for retirement or have already retired, this book offers information that can be used to make those tough decisions about your own retirement plans.

You should not be gambling with your retirement on Wall Street. Yet every day, people are led to believe that someone else has that proverbial crystal ball and will show them the way to salvation. Nothing can be further from the truth.

Some retirees know that they are gambling with their retirement on Wall Street, and others do not. That is the problem! Knowing whether or not you are gambling with your retirement is imperative to your financial well-being.

Wall Street and the present economy have changed in many ways, including some major changes over the past 10 years. For some reason, average investors think they know what Wall Street is all about; however, I am here to explain that no one really understands Wall Street and never will.

There are many unknown factors that only insiders on Wall Street know about, and even they get it wrong many times. If recent stock market crashes and pitfalls have taught us anything, it is that even the pros and insiders on Wall Street can be left confused from time to time. The stock markets are complex and volatile, and even the most experienced fund managers have been beaten by the market.

As an investor, it is important to accept some things at face value. An investor needs to obtain as much information as possible when selecting investments or products that are recommended by a so-called expert financial advisor.

Recently, Wall Street has also changed with the evolution of technology and communication, the economy, politics, and the one-world economy as well as the speed at which information can change the value of your money in an instant. As an investor, you must stay informed and educated in order to keep up with these new changes or be left behind and risk losing your money.

The most successful money managers and investors lose money every day on Wall Street, so that certainly means that the average investor can as well. It is a risk simply because no one has a crystal ball and situations do change rapidly.

As a general rule, all you can do is use your knowledge. Limit your downside by knowing as much as possible about what you are investing in or when receiving advice about buying certain products. Therefore, financial education and knowledge about retirement investing are true assets in today's financial world more than ever before.

In the movie "Wall Street," Gordon Gekko said, "If you're not inside, you're outside." This simply means education. In the movie, he was referring to illegal information which gave them an advantage in trading stock. In reality it is the same thing for the individual investor, the more you know, the better off you will be when investing for retirement.

I am sure that most of you have watched **Judge Judy** before and one of her best sayings is: **"God gave you two ears and one mouth for a reason."** That reason is to listen and learn more about something than to talk about subjects that one knows little or nothing about. That is the purpose of this chapter and, in fact, this entire book.

Listening and learning has been part of our nurturing by our parents, and this also should be part of our retirement decisions. It is necessary to be educated for the investors' benefit and success.

Years ago, people were paid for what they knew how to do, but today, people are paid for what they know. I truly believe this! In fact, my practice has become dependent on me knowing more than my competition. Clients come to me for the answers that other advisors just do not know or, frankly, do not care to know. Unfortunately, most advisors today are all about making the sale instead of helping and educating their clients first.

The problem with planning for retirement and finances in general is that it is not taught in high school or college, and for the most part, it has to be learned by trial and error — making mistakes — which can be costly.

In brief, educating yourself about your retirement or where to invest or not to invest is the first step in making the right retirement plans. With the proper education, mistakes can be limited. Fewer mistakes means more money in your pocket — period.

How the average retiree defines the meaning of retirement can be quite different today. Very few people see retirement anymore as a time when they will do nothing. People are living longer today, and that means they can work into their 70s or 80s. In South Florida, I have many clients in their 70s and 80s still working part time just so they can stay busy and earn extra cash. Making the decision to work during retirement is one thing, but having to work because you need the money is a whole other issue.

Because people are living longer, health-care costs are another factor for which a plan is needed. Many retirees forget about this and find out later how expensive health care can be without an employer assisting with the bill. Also, you need to consider long-term care in planning for retirement, as approximately 67 percent of people over 65 years old will have this type of need at some point.

Planning for retirement means educating yourself about what is needed to balance your new life during retirement. This includes planning both mentally and physically and thinking about what you will do with all the time on your hands.

There are many television commercials today asking, **"How long will your retirement last?"** This question is more important than ever because people are living longer with the advancements in medicine and medical technologies. Understanding how you make your money last as long as your life does can be interpreted quite differently from advisor to advisor. Which advisor you choose can make a big difference in the answers you will receive about this question.

The chart on **Page 5** illustrates a $500,000 lump-sum deposit earning an assumed interest rate of 5 percent per year, withdrawing $30,000 or 6 percent per year for income and deducting 25 percent for income taxes. In this example, the lump sum would completely run out of principal in year 27.

The point is that you need to know how long your money may or may not last. Running calculations to get an estimate is vital when calculating future income from your retirement funds.

Many advisors simply do not know or understand how to guarantee an income stream for the rest of a client's life. In addition, many cannot offer products such as income life annuities because their companies or broker dealers will not let them.

How Long Will Your Money Last?

YEAR	BEGINNING BALANCE	ANNUAL INTEREST @ 5%	TAXES @ 25%	WITHDRAWALS	ENDING BALANCE
1	$500,000	$24,739	$6,185	$-30,000	$488,555
2	$488,555	$24,157	$6,039	$-30,000	$476,673
3	$476,673	$23,553	$5,888	$-30,000	$464,337
4	$464,337	$22,925	$5,731	$-30,000	$451,531
5	$451,531	$22,274	$5,568	$-30,000	$438,237
6	$438,237	$21,598	$5,399	$-30,000	$424,435
7	$424,435	$20,896	$5,224	$-30,000	$410,107
8	$410,107	$20,167	$5,042	$-30,000	$395,232
9	$395,232	$19,410	$4,853	$-30,000	$379,789
10	$379,789	$18,625	$4,656	$-30,000	$363,758
11	$363,758	$17,809	$4,452	$-30,000	$347,115
12	$347,115	$16,962	$4,241	$-30,000	$329,836
13	$329,836	$16,084	$4,021	$-30,000	$311,899
14	$311,899	$15,171	$3,793	$-30,000	$293,277
15	$293,277	$14,224	$3,556	$-30,000	$273,945
16	$273,945	$13,240	$3,310	$-30,000	$253,876
17	$253,876	$12,220	$3,055	$-30,000	$233,040
18	$233,040	$11,160	$2,790	$-30,000	$211,410
19	$211,410	$10,059	$2,515	$-30,000	$188,954
20	$188,954	$8,917	$2,229	$-30,000	$165,642
21	$165,642	$7,731	$1,933	$-30,000	$141,441
22	$141,441	$6,500	$1,625	$-30,000	$116,316
23	$116,316	$5,222	$1,306	$-30,000	$90,232
24	$90,232	$3,895	$974	$-30,000	$63,154
25	$63,154	$2,518	$629	$-30,000	$35,042
26	$35,042	$1,088	$272	$-30,000	$5,858
27	$5,858	$42	$11	$-5,890	$0

A recent study was conducted by Ernst & Young. It found that three out of five middle-class retirees will run out of money if they maintain their pre-retirement lifestyles. The study also found that most retirees are just not financially prepared to make sure their money lasts as long as they do.

You have to understand that mortality rates have increased significantly because of medical advancements, and people are living much longer and this means they need to be prepared to have their money last for 30, 40 or 50 years.

Calculating how long your money will last is not that complicated. Simply account for all your money that you have saved for retirement and figure out how much you need to live off per year, then calculate the return on your money per year and divide by the number of years this money to needs last. There are free calculators online that can help you do this. Calculating the numbers is one aspect of planning for retirement, but actually finding an investment that can guarantee you income for life is another. Most financial advisors cannot guarantee you a lifetime income; in fact, the only investment that can guarantee your money for your life is an annuity. Pension plans are paid by annuities, and most large companies are doing away with these plans.

The point I am trying to make is that **"knowledge is king,"** and I am sure you have heard this before, but it is never more important than with investing your hard-earned dollars for retirement. Make sure you do not lose your money or invest in the wrong products at the wrong time without knowledge. Many people make major mistakes with their money simply because of a lack of education and experience with how to invest their life savings.

Ways to educate yourself about retirement planning:

RETIREMENT EDUCATION:

• Real Advisors	• Obtaining a Mentor (Someone successful at retirement)	• Investor Groups
• Reading		• Your Job
• Taking Classes		• Seminars & Expos
• The Internet	• Books	• Friends & Family (with no strings attached)
• Google	• The Library	
• Online Blogs	• Magazines	

A major mistake can be in selecting or choosing the wrong advisor or listening to the wrong people — those who have little or no knowledge about your retirement or your specific money needs.

Everyone has heard about **Bernie Madoff,** and if you do not get chills as an investor when I say his name, you better get a check-up! He is accountable for stealing more than $20 billion from his victims with the Ponzi scheme he used. This type of con-man is still out there preying on people every day, and you need to protect yourself.

Educating yourself is your first defense.

There should have been more people who said to themselves that Madoff's scheme was too good to be true. Unfortunately, they were seduced by their friends and families, who as a group felt safe. They listened to each other instead of professionals who knew better, and most never got a second opinion. Before anyone invested with this man, they should have done their homework. They should have called the state and federal agencies, and most importantly, they should never have given him all of their money to invest.

This can happen again, and most likely it will. But with some basic investing techniques, you can limit your downside even to thieves by **never investing all your eggs in one basket,** as most of his victims did. This was their biggest mistake of all! Why did they invest all of their money in only one investment? Is this not the golden rule to any investor — that they should follow as a precaution?

Never invest all your money in one investment!

Educating yourself is the first step to making sure you are on your way to a secure retirement plan. In addition, learning to keep away from the Bernie Madoffs of the world can be learned by education and experience.

Learn from the Rich:

We have all heard the saying, **"the rich get richer,"** but no one ever explains how or why they get richer. Here is some insight as to what that really means.

The rich, wealthy, fortunate, and affluent — or whatever else they may be called — have one thing in common. I call them well-informed.

You may want to say they are educated.

> *"You see the rich get richer because they know things that other people do not know, and they have advisors that know things that other advisors do not know."*
>
> — JOE THOMAS

More importantly they are willing to take chances with their money while limiting their downside with this knowledge.

The rich also know the value of paying less in taxes and actually growing their wealth through a selection of key tax-saving shelters, which we will talk about throughout this book. The rich and their advisors figured out a long time ago that making money is one aspect, but not being taxed on money is the most important aspect of investing for retirement.

History has shown that the government continually raises taxes over time, so finding and using the most tax-advantaged codes and concepts is one of the secrets of the rich and their great wealth. They both grow their wealth and keep that wealth intact.

Everyone has heard of a foundation from a wealthy family such as the Kennedy Foundation, the Bill Gates Foundation or the Warren Buffet Foundation or any other well-known wealthy family name set up as a foundation.

Nevertheless, this is to help people with charity and goodwill, but more importantly, the rich have found that by giving, they are receiving. What they are receiving are the biggest tax credits and protections in the U.S. tax codes.

"Rich people loathe taxes," so they also choose to live in states that have fewer taxes, especially income and estate taxes. Fewer taxes equal more money! They also seek out ways to keep their taxes as low as possible. The rich also worry about inflation and the devaluation of the dollar, so they buy investments like commercial real estate. Thus, they can depreciate assets while taking advantage of the taxes.

During the 2012 presidential election, **Mitt Romney** disclosed he had millions of dollars in off-shore accounts so he is not taxed on the money. He also has millions in **blind trusts,** which are some of the most aggressive tax-planning concepts around.

The rich use these tax laws to continue to reach their goals for wealth accumulation and legal tax reduction. There has been some debate over whether or not these tax strategies are morally or legally valid. I will tell you that if you were given advice from advisors that "know" about these tax strategies, you would be using them to the fullest extent of the law.

Rich people also choose advisors who give them real advice about tax laws and how to use these laws to the fullest advantage without going to jail. In this way, the rich not only take advantage of their earning potential but also the net effect of what they keep. This is what you should be considering each and every time you consider any investment. Ask yourself, "How can this help me tax-wise?" Look beyond just investment performance.

Techniques the rich use to stay wealthy:

No Income Means No Taxes:

If you own a business worth millions and leave the stock in the company and do not pay yourself a salary but instead borrow against the stock, then you do not have taxes. You can live quite well because you can still buy houses, cars, and boats, and the best part is that none of it is taxable, if you know how the system works.

Capital Gains Instead of Income Taxes:

This is why Warren Buffet's secretary pays more in taxes than he does. This happens simply because the rich do not pay themselves salaries that would put them in the 39.6% tax bracket but instead they have capital gains which are much lower and max out at 20 percent. As a result, they can save almost half in taxes, which is almost 50 percent fewer taxes than someone who does not have stocks and corporations. Capital gains rates are designed to encourage long-term investing. Most people can get a significant advantage from holding stock for more than one year.

TAX BRACKETS	CAPITAL GAIN TAX RATE	
	SHORT TERM	LONG TERM
10%	10%	0%
15%	15%	
25%	25%	15%
28%	28%	
33%	33%	
35%	35%	
39.6%	39.6%	20%

Delaying Taxes as Long as Possible:

The rich may be rich and wealthy on paper, but they are not taxed on their assets until they take or sell them. Let's say you own a large corporation, and you own millions of dollars in stock, buildings and real estate, but there is no tax until you sell it or use it for income. The rich do the same thing with their retirement funds. They do not touch their funds until they have to, and when they do, it is in the most tax-advantaged way possible.

Being Charitable Makes the Rich More Wealthy:

Another way the rich avoid paying taxes is to make charitable contributions. When they donate property, they never have to pay tax on that donation.

You can also donate your IRA's required minimum distribution to a charity, and you eliminate the tax completely.

Step-Up in Basis: How the Rich Families Stay Rich:

The Step-Up in Basis allows the wealthy to pass assets to their heirs even if assets have grown substantially in value without paying taxes on the gains. Stocks and real estate as well as closely held businesses can be inherited without being taxed. For example, let's say your father bought a building in the 1950s for $100,000, and now it's worth $1,000,000. When you inherit that building, you owe nothing.

Tax Deferred vs. Taxable vs. Tax Free:

Taxes are all about bottom-line results. The final result of what you made or what you earned, and nothing else really matters when it comes to money and investing.

All qualified retirement plans are tax-deferred, which means you will pay taxes eventually. Taxable means you will always pay taxes, like it or not. Tax free simply means you never pay taxes. Knowing which one of these tax considerations to choose can mean a substantial difference in wealth accumulation. Most advisors will tell you it is all about the returns, but I am here to tell you it is all about the taxes. You need to invest in products or retirement plans that limit, reduce or do not have taxes associated with their growth. This is one key area that distinguishes the rich from the uninformed investor.

The rich listen to what advisors have to say and their recommendations. Then they act on it when the time is right without the pressure of a pushy salesman. Therefore, they act when deciding to act, not when an advisor tells them to. This alone can increase your success rate significantly. The rich value the fact that they make decisions when the time is right for them and not someone else.

The rich also discuss money issues with each other and therefore learn things others do not. They can learn from each other with how to make and keep more money. They also openly discuss money issues and concepts with their children and teach them from a very young age. They use trust and legal instruments that their valued advisors recommend to their fullest advantage.

Most people are more likely to talk about their sex lives with a total stranger than they are to talk about their money, mainly because people fear money in many ways. Usually, people either do not want someone to know how much money they do or do not have. This is because you may have more than them or, worse, you may want to borrow money from them.

Keeping secrets about your money is not a great idea if you want your money to do well. Being open-minded and discussing your money and goals is a "good thing," as Martha Stewart says. Please keep in mind; I am not advising you to tell the world about your net worth. Make sure you understand that. I propose that you talk openly about your money to your most trusted advisors or other knowledgeable people who can help guide you.

In this way, they can help identify your best plan of action. You can learn from talking about different types of investing techniques others may be using. Even some of my own clients will not tell me about all of their assets, because it is just the way they protect their money — by keeping a wall up to protect it. I can tell you from my experience that the most up-front clients disclose all of their money so that their advisor can make more educated, informed recommendations.

There is also a big fallacy in this country that we should act like the rich even if we are not rich. Children today are being taught this by their parents, unfortunately. There is an attitude in this country today called: "Spend it first with credit and pay later for the rest of your life" or "fake it till you make it" mentality.

Unfortunately, this is not beneficial and will be the downfall of many people who follow this way of life. This belief with how to handle money can be devastating and as a result many Americans have huge money issues today because of these beliefs. Debt is good in some respects and, without it, many people cannot accomplish some of the things they need to do, but ask savvy seniors if they have a mortgage or have a car loan or owe serious amounts of money to a credit card company, and the answer is, "No."

Maybe the younger generation needs to take a lesson from older, wiser people who have been there and done that — spend less and save more. It is important not to buy something before you can actually afford to buy it. This is good advice and more importantly a learning process. If there is one thing my wealthiest clients have taught me, it is that in order to make millions, you have to save millions first. Thus by not spending it before you make it is the way to accumulate it and not the other way around.

My opinion on the bottom line is to educate yourself first then talk to others who know something and evaluate things for yourself. When making tough retirement decisions, take your time and learn the available options without making hasty choices.

I wish I had a dime for every time I have heard someone say, **"It's Greek to me,"** because nothing should be misunderstood when it comes to your money. By educating yourself, you can understand how anything with your money works. You must make the time to educate yourself before you invest or speak to an advisor who can interpret "Greek" into dollars and cents.

It is my belief that people say, "It's Greek to me," so they do not have the responsibility for their own foolish mistakes. It is your money, and you are responsible for all the mistakes you make or that someone else you hire makes with your money.

Refrain from the excuses like "It's Greek to me," or better yet, **"If it's too good to be true, it probably is."** This is just another excuse from people who cannot understand that you need to be savvy with your money — which means educated.

The rich (well-informed) learn and educate themselves about complicated topics on retirement and taxes so they can benefit from this information. Then they take advantage by using that information to move forward with their financial plans.

The most important reason you need to educate yourself about your money is so that you understand and can make the determination whether you are receiving good advice or bad advice from your advisors.

As you know, life is an education process that may take you time to understand. Some of these financial concepts and products are difficult to understand, but you did not learn to walk without crawling first. The right advisor can be there for you by educating you with these financial topics.

Anything that has to do with your money that you may buy or invest in should be clear, and if you do not understand it, then learn about it or find someone who can explain it to you before you invest. It is your money, so you'd better talk dollars and cents.

Another excuse I have heard before is, **"What you don't know can't hurt you."** This is false when it comes to investing your money. You had better know as much as you can, or it will hurt you and come back to cause you problems later.

Some people today from the middle class to the very wealthy go through life guessing at what they should be doing. It is my belief that the ones with the most knowledge do better than those that do not have a clue. You may get lucky once or twice, but the people who educate themselves about their money do better in the short and long run than those who do not.

Understanding that the middle class work for their money and that the rich have their money work for them can mean significant gains in your retirement.

A perfect example is that my wealthiest clients have taught me that you should never leave money sitting around in a checking account at ridiculously low rates waiting for interest rates to go up, like many people are doing today.

The well-educated clients are looking and searching for the opportunities that are available right now so they can maximize their returns on all their money. There is a big distinction in understanding this as an investor.

Thinking like the rich may be imperative to all types of investors, rich or otherwise. This simply means that the rich have learned shortcuts to putting their money to work for them. Therefore, when they make money, they look at it differently than uneducated people do.

For example, the uneducated get their paycheck, and before they get it, they think about what they can buy with it. When their tax return comes, they think about putting a deposit on a new car or new boat that they can finance. In contrast, the rich think about how they can invest that same money to make their money grow. Also, they make more money by not spending it but instead by saving it while limiting taxes.

Two Sets of Laws:

In my opinion, there are basically **two sets of laws in this country; one for the informed and one for the uninformed.** If you do not think this is true, you may be sadly mistaken. Knowing which set of laws to choose can be life-changing for your retirement.

Judge Learned Hand was one of the greatest judges in America in his time. He started out as a Teddy Roosevelt Republican and ended up a Roosevelt Democrat. He was a famed American judge and an avid supporter of free speech, though he is most remembered for applying economic reasoning to American tort law. Hand is generally considered to be one of the most influential American judges ever to have served on the Supreme Court of the United States.

> *"Anyone may arrange his affairs so that his taxes shall be as low as possible; he is not bound to choose that pattern which best pays the Treasury. There is not even a patriotic duty to increase one's taxes. Over and over again, the courts have said that there is nothing sinister in so arranging affairs as to keep taxes as low as possible. Everyone does it, rich and poor alike and all do right, for nobody owes any public duty to pay more than the law demands."*
>
> — JUDGE LEARNED HAND

This simply means to find out the answers to reducing taxes like the rich do because it will help you grow your money faster and it will last longer. Educate yourself so you are on the right side of this law. If not, then you will be left behind in many respects.

We all have said to ourselves, "If I only knew then what I know now," things would have been different. Right? Of course!

This is why Mitt Romney uses these tax laws to his advantage, and there is no moral obligation to anyone — including the government. Fewer taxes mean you are doing your best job to protect yourself and your rights as an American.

Ask yourself, "How can you know to do something in the future?" The answer is by educating yourself as much as you can! Education will change your future results positively. Your retirement success depends on the level of education you have and how you use it to choose the direction with the plans, advisors and types of investments you make.

More importantly, the taxes you may save on by choosing certain plans or advisors can determine your retirement success or failure. Learning this may take some skill and time but can be accomplished by anyone.

There is a direct correlation between the returns you will reap and the success rate you will achieve, which can all be attributed to your level of financial education. More education equals fewer mistakes which equals more money in your pocket. The decisions you make, whether good or bad, will directly affect the success you have with your retirement plan. Your self-education will also prepare you so you can talk with and learn from the advisors you may choose. Education will help you to make better retirement decisions when choosing an advisor, as well.

Remember it is not what you know only, but it is also about what you do with what you know that can make the difference!

The next chapter will discuss how to choose an **advisor** who is right for you. Also, you will learn how to know the difference between an advisor who is helping you with your money and one who is helping themselves to your money.

2

ADVISORS

Advisor: *a person who gives advice; typically someone who is an expert in a particular field.*

My definition adds this: **"Has the heart of a teacher** and will help teach you the basics you need to know so you have a general understanding of what investment choices you should be considering."

This advisor has your best interest in mind — not theirs. Remember the advisor gives advice and is an expert in their particular field.

> *"Wall Street is the place people drive to in their Rolls Royce to take advice from people who ride the subway!"*
>
> — WARREN BUFFET

You may want to read this again, because it is so true! Understanding this can truly enlighten your perspective with the relationship between you and your advisor. Also it can make a huge difference in what advice you take or do not take.

There are many **different types of advisors** available. I am not going to explain or endorse which one is better than another, for in my opinion, they are all useful in their own ways. It is ultimately up to the individual how to use them and evaluate them for the specific situation at hand!

In my opinion, titles are good. However, they are more important to the advisor who holds the title than to the client, who may not understand the title anyway. Most investors do not understand, and most do not care. A fancy title does not ensure high standards or even correct advice; some titles are earned, while others are purchased. In my opinion, ethics are more important.

Neither the Securities and Exchange Commission nor the North American Securities Administrators Association endorses any financial professional titles. They encourage the client to look beyond a title to determine whether the advisor can provide the type of financial services or products needed. Do not rely solely on the title to determine whether a financial professional has the expertise that is necessary.

Secondly, you must choose an advisor based on individual needs to solve the issue at hand, and this means finding a true expert or specialist in that field. The client may also prefer to pick a male or female advisor, but this is purely based on personal preference.

In my opinion, the biggest danger to any consumer is the fact that most consumers do not know who they are dealing with at first. The greatest risk is that of being misled into thinking that this advisor is acting in your best interest rather than the advisor's best interest. This happens more often than you know.

The difference between brokers and advisors, and between salesmen and advisors, is usually determined by the advice you receive based on how they are paid. This advice will vary greatly based on this one criterion.

I believe **all advisors** no matter their title should have a **fiduciary responsibility** to each and every client with whom they do business. Fiduciary responsibility means that the advisor is on your side and has a responsibility to recommend what is best for you and your finances regardless of the impact on the advisor's own income.

Next, I also believe that any advisor making a recommendation to a client about purchasing any investment, insurance, retirement or other financial product first and foremost should make sure that those recommendations are suitable to the client.

The advisor should consider your risk tolerance, overall needs, investment objectives, tax considerations, your prior experience and appetite for risk. Also, he or she needs to help make the right recommendations that are suitable to each and every client as needed.

Suitability means that the product is right for you. Does it fit your needs, and does it meet your overall need to purchase this product? Are you financially fit to buy this product based on the advisor's recommendation?

As I mentioned before, my opinion is that ethics play a major role in choosing the right advisor. This is because ethics tell you something about how the advisor may act as an ethical person giving you advice that will not harm or hurt you.

The Million Dollar Round Table Code of Ethics:

Members of the Million Dollar Round Table should be ever mindful that complete compliance with and observance of the Code of Ethics of the Million Dollar Round Table shall serve to promote the highest-quality standards of membership. These standards will be beneficial to the public and the insurance and financial services profession.

Therefore, each member shall:

- Always place the best interests of their clients above their own direct or indirect interests.

- Maintain the highest standards of professional competence and give the best possible advice to clients by seeking to maintain and improve professional knowledge, skills and competence.

- Hold in strictest confidence, and consider as privileged, all business and personal information pertaining to their clients' affairs. Make full and adequate disclosure of all facts necessary to enable clients to make informed decisions.

- Maintain personal conduct that will reflect favorably on the insurance and financial services profession and MDRT.

- Determine that any replacement of an insurance or financial product must be beneficial for the client.

- Abide by and conform to all provisions of the laws and regulations in the jurisdictions in which they do business.

Remember the most important thing about advisors is that **you pick them,** so do not complain if they perform badly or do not adhere to what you expected. Remember clients chose to use Bernie Madoff, not the other way around. For example, if you do not want to invest your money in risky investments, then do not choose a risky advisor who sells and recommends risky investments.

You need to pick an advisor who invests your money as if it is your money and not theirs! This means the age of the advisor and their experience may determine the results received as well as the level of risk with the investments recommended.

For example, if an investor is 65 years old and the advisor is 30 years old, you may be getting advice based on a 30-year-old's view of investing and not that of a retired or soon-to-be retired investor age 65 who needs safety in a portfolio. It is crucial to make sure your advisor has a certain level of experience, and how the advisor looks at your money is also very important.

If you do not hear what you want to hear from your advisor, then get another advisor. Many people think they are stuck with their advisors because they are intimidated to make a change, but believe me, **change is good** and can make the biggest difference in the world. It entails having the right advisor — even if this means breaking ties with a longtime advisor who is not working out.

Very importantly, your advisor works for you! You need to be in control, not the other way around! **Never give up control of your money!** Understand that you are the one who selects the advisor and you can terminate your relationship if he or she does not live up to your goals or specific financial needs.

My advice is this: If you cannot sleep at night because you are worried about the risky investments you own, get out of them by changing your risky advisor. Many clients feel some type of personal commitment to their advisor, but understand this is not your priest, pastor or rabbi. It is your money and is about how well the advisor fits your needs, not the other way around. Please remember there is nothing personal here. It is just business.

In this situation, we are not talking about hurting someone's feelings. We are talking about life or death as it relates to your economic future, your money, your families' money and your future livelihood. As an investor, you should never make investment or retirement decisions based on emotions or feelings, especially when it comes to the advisors with whom you work. Your advisor is a tool such as any other investment or retirement tool you may use that helps you accomplish your goals for retirement.

I have had clients complain to me about their advisors, and some cannot seem to cut ties when they should get a second opinion. A second opinion can make all the difference in great success or failure for an investor. Obtaining a second opinion can also give you a new perspective on your investments and move you toward your retirement goals faster. Let us discuss what a **second opinion** really means when it comes to selecting another advisor or the reviewing of your finances by a different advisor. Getting a second opinion means you need to get it from a new source. This does not mean to call the same person from whom you have been receiving advice in the past.

Never get a second opinion from the person who already advised you in the past; get someone new. This way you can compare, and decide if that new advisor fits your needs and investment beliefs or future plans.

In addition, you may want to use an additional advisor to advise you in certain areas, in which your original advisor just is not knowledgeable. Choose a new advisor to manage only a certain asset or percentage of your money as you see fit. Never see your current advisor as an all-or-nothing type of situation, as that is not good for your financial success.

When interviewing for a new advisor, you need to ask questions and give them the third degree, just like **Sgt. Friday from the classic TV show "Dragnet," who said, "The facts, Ma'am; nothing but the facts."**

If you were told you needed surgery, wouldn't you get a second opinion from another doctor? Of course you would! Your life may depend on that second opinion. **When your money is involved, your financial life does depend on it. So get a second or even a third opinion, because it is that important.**

I recommend that you interview with two or three advisors until you find one that fits your needs and risk tolerance. Tell them up front that you are interviewing and that you will not be making any final decisions until you have made a choice.

The biggest benefits of a second opinion are getting your most important questions answered and evaluating changes that may need to be made. You can also use second opinions to form a consensus as to what you are doing is correct or it may warrant a change.

Keep in mind, things change, and so should your planning techniques and advisors — if warranted — from year to year or problem to problem. When choosing an advisor, if your advisor makes a mistake with your money it is your money and not theirs, so they do not lose anything, only you do! When searching for a new advisor an investor needs to know what that advisor specializes in and you can find out simply by asking them.

Certain advisors handle different financial aspects and recommend different products or services. As a result, you need to know what they do so you can decide if they can help you with your specific needs.

In my opinion, this is why titles do not matter with advisors because they may only specialize in one area and you may use them for that area only. What difference would it make if he or she has a title or not? (It is like comparing regular gas with premium gas. They are still both gas. One has a better title, but they both get you where you want to go.)

The reason you want to know the advisor's specialty is to obtain an advisor who specifically fits the advice you seek. For example, if you have an advisor who specializes in bonds and you want to invest in stocks, then this advisor may not be for you.

Here is what I recommend you should do before you meet with any advisor:

- Write down your questions before the advisor arrives.
- Write down your goals for the money.
- Write down any issues or problems you may have.
- Discuss with your significant other his or her goals.
- Prepare all your financial statements according to where your money is located, so that the advisor can evaluate and make recommendations.

Tell the advisor what you are looking for; more income, less income, reducing taxes, paying off mortgage, saving for college, retiring at a certain age or whatever it is you want to accomplish. Find out what the advisors would recommend to solve your problems at hand.

Next, be prepared to not make any hasty decisions, but instead evaluate the advisors' recommendations and decide one or two days later. They may tell you, "This plan won't be here tomorrow." If this happens, then your response should be, "Good, then it was not right for me!" Keep in mind, at this point that you are talking and learning who the advisors are and how much experience they have. You are also finding out how the advisors work and what he or she knows to solve your problems or reach your goals.

Ask the potential advisor the following questions:
- In what do you specialize?
- Who are your ideal clients?
- What is your minimum client's net worth?
- What is your minimum amount to open an account?
- What products/services do you sell or offer?
- What products are you not able to offer?
- What titles do you have?
- How long have you been doing this?
- In what do you invest?
- How do you get paid?
- How are you licensed by the state or federal government?
- What are your license numbers?
- Who do I call to check out your license?
- Do you have any references I can call?
- Do you have any sample plans you have done?
- What's your own investment philosophy?
- Will I be dealing with you or an assistant?
- Do you have a fiduciary capacity to your clients?

- How long have you been at this firm?
- How long were you at your last firm?
- Do you have any infractions or violations on your license?

It may even be wise to ask them about their political beliefs; I believe it is all fair when choosing your advisor for your hard-earned money! I have been asked so many personal questions that it does not even bother me anymore. If it bothers someone you are interviewing, then find another advisor.

After you have met with the advisor, now is the time to do your due diligence. This means going to work on checking him or her out. Call the state; call the feds; call referrals he or she gave you, and call the companies the advisors are recommending. Now is the time to check them out thoroughly.

Check if an advisor is licensed and legal:

This is who to call to find out if your advisor is licensed and legally doing business. There are basically two ways: either federally licensed or state licensed.

Federal License check for Advisors Selling Securities:

FINRA: Financial Industry Regulatory Authority
Phone Number: 301-590-6500
Online: www.BrokerCheck.Finra.org/search

Your advisor may be regulated by the Securities and Exchange Commission, which is responsible for ensuring fairness for the individual investor. FINRA is responsible for overseeing virtually all U.S. stockbrokers and brokerage firms. FINRA is overseen by the SEC.

Financial Advisors Selling Insurance Products:

Call the State Department of Insurance or Professional License Departments and ask for a License Check.

New York: 800-342-3736
California: 800-927-4357
Florida: 877-693-5236

Just because one advisor is licensed by the state and another is licensed by the feds does not make one better than the other. Each licensed advisor should be accepted for what they know and what recommendations they are making in their field of expertise.

Keep in mind some advisors today wear many hats, and you must be diligent in finding out what they do and how they can or cannot help you. Also make sure that you have different advisors that do different things for you, especially when it comes to your retirement money.

One advisor doing it all for you is not good practice. You may want several advisors helping you with advice for your retirement.

Some advisors claim to specialize in retirement, but many do not. **Some just push products** and do not plan, and others say they have plans and do not push products. Ultimately, you need to be the judge of what they can do for you and not the other way around. Understand that no one can be a specialist or expert in everything, so as smart as your present advisor may be, he or she does not know everything about all financial matters.

When talking about advisors, we need to talk about accountants, as they are not the end-all to the advice you should be receiving when it comes to your retirement planning. Most are very nice people, but let's face it, they prepare your taxes with a computer program. They may be good with numbers, but this does not mean they know anything about investing or retirement planning. Many of them pretend to know by giving you the wrong advice, which can hurt you even more.

My experience with accountants is that they can either be too aggressive or too conservative in the wrong places. They need to be used for the type of advisor they are. They prepare your taxes and can advise about the tax implications on the tax deductibility on certain retirement accounts. On the other hand, there are many good accountants who are priceless because they are actually advising clients on taxes and how to use the tax code to the fullest advantage of the law. A knowledgeable accountant can be invaluable.

There are also some accountants today who are representing clients as both an accountant and as a financial advisor, and in my opinion, this may present a conflict of interest.

As to advisors and which to choose, you may want one person to handle your IRA and another to handle your 401(k). The point I am making is that each plan, product or advice may require a different advisor.

Many clients prefer to have one firm, broker or advisor advising them on all their money needs, and you need to be aware that this is not practical in the real world of retirement today!

How do you know if this advisor believes in what he or she offers? How do you know if he or she is as experienced or reputable as they say they are? Ask them!

I show my clients what retirement plans I own and invest in so they know I believe in the products. Ask what other clients are doing or buying, if you will be his biggest client or his smallest client as this may make a huge difference with the level of advice and promptness you receive.

The next quote is so important. Read it twice. Think about it: if an advisor knows so much about "making money in the stock market or with the advice they give" he or she would not be selling and asking for your money because they would have no time; instead they would be investing and managing their own money.

> *"The reason they are called brokers is because they are broker than you."*
>
> — ROBERT KIYOSAKI,
> AUTHOR OF "RICH DAD, POOR DAD"

Recently, I had a potential client who came into my office to discuss moving over his retirement account from another advisor. During our conversation about the other advisor, the client made a comment that really epitomizes this chapter with regard to picking the right advisor.

He said, "My present advisor drives a new BMW; "that's how successful he is."

The client's perception had nothing to do with how well his advisor had done with his retirement account or the advice he may have given him, but the client's opinion was based on the perception that this advisor was successful because he drove a BMW. I told the client that the advisor probably leases his car. Your perception can get in the way sometimes when choosing an advisor.

The reason I am revealing this is because most advisors do not have any real assets or investments to speak of. They are doing this because they need to make a living, and they need your money to make money. Just understand who is providing advice about money.

This simply means before you take any advice, you need to know the difference between a sales pitch and sound investment advice! Your job is to know the difference, because it is your money at stake not theirs!

The most trusted advisors you have presently may not be the ones you really need to advise you on your retirement. You may trust them, but they might not really understand every aspect as it relates to your best interests.

Trust is another area we need to clarify. It should not be the only factor in deciding to use an advisor. For instance, many people trusted Bernie Madoff, yet he stole billions. You need to understand how to use certain advisors for certain situations, even though you may trust one more than another.

By having different advisors, you are spreading risk, as each advisor has different investment philosophies that can help limit losses through different investment products. Just as you would spread your investment risk to prevent losses, if you spread your advisors out and use them for different products or services, you are spreading your risk even further.

Types of Advisors:
- Retirement Planner
- Financial Planner
- CPA/Accountant

- Attorney
- Tax Attorney
- Insurance Agent
- Stock Broker
- Brokerage Account Broker
- Banker
- Bank Broker
- **Friends, Family, Neighbors and Know-it-alls**

Be careful with the **free advice** you receive, because most of the time it is wrong, bad or biased. The advice you receive may also be based on what's best for the person giving you the advice and not for you.

Certain advisors should be used separately and independently of each other. Some you may use together and others individually. Understand what each one specializes in and see if they fit your overall retirement plan. You can take in free advice from some of them, but ultimately, YOU make the decision, not them.

When you are attempting to solve an issue or problem at hand, you need an expert or **problem solver** who can educate you as to your needs. A problem solver may be an advisor in his or her area of specialty and not someone moonlighting. This specifically means to not use the "know it all's" for areas of specialty that they may not have the experience or knowledge. Ask the potential advisor who their "perfect client" is before you start to do business with them, and see if you fit.

Advisor Categories

Stock Brokers

They handle stock transactions. They sell securities, which include stocks, bonds, mutual funds and other securities their broker-dealer may offer. They they work with and are employed by the broker-dealer. They are regulated by the SEC and FINRA, and they are known as registered representatives, or registered reps. They are paid commissions.

Investment Advisors

These are individuals or companies who are paid for providing advice about securities. They offer tailored advice through their products.

They are regulated the same as stock brokers by the SEC and FINRA. Investment advisors are also known as asset managers, investment counselors and managers, portfolio managers and wealth managers. They can be paid hourly, at a fixed rate, on commission from the products they offer, as a percentage of the assets you invest or a combination of all of the above.

Financial, Retirement, Estate and Insurance Planners

They help individuals meet their goals by providing services such as: asset allocation, estate, insurance, retirement, risk management and tax planning. They can be a stock broker or investment advisor, insurance agents or practicing accountants. These planners are regulated by both the state and the feds in most cases, but sometimes one or the other. They are paid by a fee or commission.

The bottom line is that stock brokers, investment advisors and financial planners come from a variety of educational and professional backgrounds. Some of their jobs overlap each other and some do similar jobs so it is important to decide what you are doing first before you chose just one because you might use all three.

Unfortunately, we live in a world of **know-it-alls,** and some of these people may be uneducated when it comes to finances. Everyone seems to have an opinion, whether right or wrong, and that is the American way in many respects. However, you need to be realistic about who can help and advise you with your money and have your best interest in mind and not theirs. This is paramount to your survival.

When I meet with a new client, I often ask what the client does or did for a living, and quite often my clients had substantial careers. Some were doctors, lawyers, dentists, engineers, teachers, professors, and managers. Many of them held occupations I had never even heard of or know very little about.

Since I generally know little about the complexities of their jobs, I tell them, "I know nothing about your occupation, but I do know about finances and retirement." They understand that no one person can be an expert on everything including retirement planning. On the other hand, this does not mean there are not clients who know as much as I do about retirement planning — but they do not know it all.

I had a client who called me and told me that his new son-in-law said that the plan I had implemented for them more than 10 years before was completely wrong. I asked, "What does your new son-in-law do for a living?" They client told me the son-in-law was an auto mechanic. Obviously, I have nothing against mechanics, but the comparison of his knowledge to mine was an insult in many respects.

If my client told me that he was some type of professional who has knowledge and expertise that warranted his opinion, I would most definitely have accepted it. Generally, most in-laws or family members (in my experience) are looking out for what is best for themselves and not what is best for their in-laws.

Your son or daughter or whoever is helping you may be looking at your money as if it is theirs and not yours. How you look at money determines how you invest your money. As an advisor, they should be looking at your money through your eyes and not theirs.

Perhaps your son or daughter may want you to purchase stocks or mutual funds because they are younger and would have time to recoup losses if the market goes down. However, instead it would be better for you to purchase a safer, more stable product such as fixed annuities or government bonds that are more suitable to your needs for income as opposed to their needs. How your money is viewed by others is extremely important, and you need to realize this.

As far as the son-in-law, I told the client to tell the son-in-law to continue being a mechanic and I would continue to be a retirement advisor since I possess more than 30 years of experience. Fortunately, that was the end of the conversation as the client understood what I was saying and everything remained as it had before.

Some people are very naïve when it comes to finances, and many take advice initially from people they know and trust. Instead, they should try to find real advisors who can help them with unbiased knowledge and experience when making retirement planning decisions.

It is my recommendation to my clients that they bring their family members along with them if they feel they need to, so they can participate in making decisions, **but many of the people you think want to help you with your money also want to help themselves to your money.** It is crucial to be careful with the source of your advice and what the real motives are in third party intentions.

How you look at money may be very different than how someone else looks at your money!

A very rich man and his wife were staying at an upscale hotel in Hollywood, California. He and his wife decided to have lunch. They stopped at the local store and bought some apples, a piece of cheese, some crackers and a few drinks. They drove back to the hotel, sat on the porch of the hotel in an area with the best view overlooking the mountains and the beach.

While they sat there eating their lunch, their son, who was in his 30s, pulled up with his new, shiny, fire-engine red Corvette. He flew up, jumped out of the car and tossed the valet his keys, saying, "Park it, buddy." After the valet parked his car, he went over to the parents sitting on the porch of the hotel and asked, "Why are you sitting here at one of the fanciest hotels in Hollywood, eating apples and cheese, when your son is driving a brand new, shiny, red Corvette?" The man answered, "You see, sir, my son has a millionaire for a father, and I don't!"

Your advice and plans for your money should also evolve and change as you age or circumstances change, such as death, divorce, marriage, the economy, Wall Street, market conditions, and interest rates. This includes any change that could affect your money in any way. As your situations in life change, you may need to change advisors as well.

Change is also a good thing, although I am a firm believer in the saying, **"If it ain't broke, don't fix it."** As long as you are happy with your situation and nothing major has happened to warrant a change in your plan or advice, do not make changes.

Life events that may warrant changes:

- Inheritance
- New baby
- Marriage (yours or a family members)
- Divorce (yours or a family members)
- Home Buying or Selling
- Moving
- Loss of Spouse or Loved One
- Job Loss
- Retirement
- Downsizing
- Financial Needs
- Economic Conditions
- World Politics
- Any change that may affect your money

Each and every one of these events in life may warrant a change in the way you view your retirement plans. Changes may be necessary accordingly.

It is critical to understand the difference between a **real advisor** and a **fake advisor.** The way to do this is by interviewing several advisors for different uses of your money. They must have the "heart of a teacher." They must educate you. If they do not, do not use them. Ask questions and remember that no question is a stupid question if you do not know the answer!

There are even fake advisors on television or the radios, on stations such as CNN, CNBC and FOX, for example. Please realize these people on television are paid actors and journalists, acting out their advice about the market, the economy, and other scenarios as it relates to ratings for the television show. They do not know any more than you do about financial topics, and in many cases, they may know less, so be very cautious. They are not professional, experienced advisors; usually they are personalities and journalists expressing their opinions about finance and money.

I watch many of these shows and enjoy them, but I am looking for information and entertainment, not for solid financial advice. You need to be able to filter the good from the bad and not be influenced by acting skills and empty opinions.

I actually have had clients who have called me after watching some of these shows and told me that "Suze Orman told me to do this or that." This has happened several times.

Let's be realistic here. Just because someone is on television does not not mean they know it all when it comes to everything that has to do with money, especially in the case of Suze Orman. I like her for how she promotes taking charge of your money and some of the other concepts she promotes, but I do not care for her lack of diversity with investing and more specifically that she only recommends buying stock no matter the individual needs.

Dave Ramsey is another advisor who only professes one type of investing — to buy only mutual funds and stocks for your retirement. This is just not good practical sense when it comes to investing for retirement.

Sometimes people on television work in the financial world, but they have their own hidden agendas and best interests in mind, not yours. Basically, they want the market to do well so they do well, yet they do not have any interest in the least as to what happens to you or your money. Most of their comments are made to a broad audience so they get away with this bad advice all the time. You need to look past it or not even watch it at all.

Key points about TV advisors like Suze Orman, Dave Ramsey and Jim Cramer: They do not know you, and they are making generalizations to a mass audience. They have no idea what your specific needs may or may not be.

Most of the advice they give is very general. Realize that you are unique in your age, risk tolerance, amount of assets you have to invest and what goals you want to accomplish with your finances.

These TV personalities are promoting their books, programs and third-party endorsements. Because there is money involved, they are not going to veer from their motives.

Keep in mind that investing in the stock market in stocks or mutual funds is not for everyone, and common sense should dictate that. There is no one-size-fits-all investing approach, and especially not when it comes to the level of risk you are willing to invest. This decision should be based only upon your view and not that of someone on television.

Ultimately, you should understand more than anything else is that these TV advisors are entertainers first and foremost, so accept it for what it is.

Next we need to discuss **advisors versus customer service representatives.** This is another area in which to be careful. Knowing who you are talking with and receiving advice from on the phone is important.

How can you tell if the person on the other end of the phone is an advisor giving you advice or a customer service representative giving you opinions that do not matter? Ask! It is vital to know!

Ask them if they are licensed to be providing you with this information, advice or recommendations. In addition, you may also ask them if they can be held accountable for their advice. They will say most likely that they cannot!

Beware of this when you call financial companies, such as Fidelity, Charles Schwab, Scottrade, or any company that you call and speak with a customer service representative.

Often you are speaking with people who have no licenses, little experience and — in most cases — know very little about investing! Some of these "so-called-experts" may even be in another country, yet everyday these people are giving you and others unprofessional opinions about your money!

Know that the people you talk with may not be advisors in the capacity you may think. Again, the burden is on you — the client — to figure this out. Not knowing to whom you are talking can cost you time and money.

Good Advisor, Bad Advice:

I wrote an article titled, "Good Advisor, Bad Advice" around 2001 after one of the major crashes in the stock market. The point of it was that so many good advisors were simply giving their clients bad advice.

What I meant by this was that the advisors kept telling clients to keep buying and investing, even though the stock market was going through a significant correction.

The real picture was that good advisors may be nice people, and you might trust them, but it does not mean you need to listen to them all the time. Remember it is your money, and hard decisions need to be made from time to time — with or without them.

Why would your broker or advisor tell you to keep buying and not sell your stock when the market is correcting? This could be because they would not make any money if they told you to sell and buy something safer!

This leads to the consequences of **bad advice.** Make sure you understand that the advice you receive from your advisor greatly depends on their background, knowledge, experience and education. Some advisors give bad advice based on these factors. Also, understand that advisors want to help you make the right decisions about your money, but they are directly compensated by those decisions. For some advisors, self-interest may come first, and this can create a conflict with what is best for you.

Beware of good advisors with bad advice, such as:
- Not selling and taking the loss when you should.
- Not being realistic about market conditions.
- Picking products that benefit advisor more than you.
- Excessive trading & churning that only the advisor.
- Leverage your accounts with margin trading.
- Selling high-cost investments only.
- Not telling you what you really need to know.
- Not understanding the products they are offering.
- Being too optimistic about real market conditions.
- Poorly diversified portfolio.

Bad advice does occur with some very good advisors (that you may trust) which can result in poor performance and loss of value for you the investor, thus beware and stay alert when selecting the right advisor for your retirement money.

This brings us to our next chapter on the **costs** associated with retirement plans.

3

COSTS: *FEES, INFLATION & TAXES*

Hidden Costs *exist that many advisors and investors do not know about or even discuss. Before making any investment decisions about retirement, these costs should be explored. These hidden costs are so blatant and costly that if you do not plan for them, you will be the only one that pays the price.*

"Money often costs too much."

— RALPH WALDO EMERSON

First, let us define these costs individually:

- **Fees:** A payment made to a professional person or to a professional or public body in exchange for advice or services.
- **Inflation:** In economics, a sustained increase in the general price level of goods and services in an economy over a period of time.
- **Taxes:** A sum of money demanded by a government for its support or for specific facilities or services, such as those levied upon incomes, property, and sales.

Fees, taxes and inflation; these are three of the most important costs that anyone planning for retirement should understand prior to initiating any retirement plan. It is unfortunate that many advisors only discuss how well the returns are going to perform, when instead they should be planning how much you will net after these costs are deducted.

Your bottom line — similar to the bottom line of the wealthy — should not only be about what you earn but instead what you keep and continue to grow. That means reducing costs whenever possible. These costs are hard to completely remove; however, their impact can be limited by knowing about them and planning for them. You can make a big difference in your bottom line simply by being aware of these costs before investing in certain products or plans over others.

There is a huge difference in retirement planning, between what you earn and what you keep! This is better known as **gross versus net**. You need to know the difference!

The difference is called **real return.** Many investors and advisors are unaware of how this works, but it is simple once you know. **Real return is what is left after you subtract taxes and inflation.**

If advisors are only looking at nominal returns when building a portfolio, they are ignoring the impact of inflation, taxes and expenses which can hurt your future growth and expectations. You should subtract these fees as an estimate when possible.

The chart on page 39 shows the real returns of certificates of deposit over the 25 years from 1974 to 1998. The reason I picked these dates is because I have many clients who tell me how well CDs paid in the late 1970s. They were earning 10 percent to 16 percent, but they never accounted for taxes and inflation. For example, in 1979, the average CD rate was 11.2 percent, the highest tax rate was 59 percent, and inflation was 13.3 percent. When you deduct taxes and inflation, the real return was actually -8.7 percent, meaning they lost money. Understanding real return can make a true difference in your retirement presently and in the future.

It is important to find an advisor who discusses how to keep more of the money earned after these costs are deducted. Remembering that net is more important than gross and knowing about your real returns is imperative to your success for retirement.

Fees:
- Broker Fees
- Commissions
- Management Fees
- Hidden Fees (which are invisible but exist)
- Maintenance Fees

Real CD Returns
25-Year History

YEAR	CD RATE (%)	LESS TAXES (%)	LESS INFLATION (%)	REAL RETURN AFTER TAXES & INFLATION (%)
1974	6.9	62	12.4	-9.8
1975	6.9	62	6.9	-4.3
1976	5.6	62	4.9	-2.8
1977	5.9	60	6.7	-4.3
1978	8.2	60	9.0	-5.7
1979	11.2	59	13.3	-8.7
1980	13.3	59	12.5	-7.0
1981	16.3	59	8.9	-2.2
1982	13.8	50	3.8	3.1
1983	9.5	48	3.8	1.1
1984	10.9	45	3.9	2.1
1985	8.8	45	3.8	1.0
1986	7.0	45	1.1	2.8
1987	6.8	33	4.4	0.2
1988	7.8	33	4.4	0.8
1989	9.6	33	4.7	1.7
1990	8.6	31	6.3	-0.4
1991	6.6	31	2.7	1.9
1992	4.3	31	3.1	-0.1
1993	3.4	36	2.7	-0.5
1994	4.6	36	2.7	0.2
1995	6.3	36	2.6	1.4
1996	5.7	36	3.4	0.2
1997	5.5	36	1.7	1.8
1998	5.4	36	1.8	1.6

CD rates are 6-mo. annualized average monthly rates; taxes are based on federal tax only at the $150,000 level; inflation is based on the Consumer Price Index.

If your money is Qualified (IRA/401(k)/annuity) then you will not have taxes until you withdraw the money, but eventually you will pay taxes on the money.

- Expense Fees
- Transaction Fees
- Front-End and Rear-End Load Fees
- Custodian Fees
- Plan Administration Fees

In my opinion, the biggest fee or expense occurs when you do not have an advisor who knows about these hidden costs. (Having one who advises how to cope, plan, reduce or eliminate them from your retirement plan is essential and priceless.)

Other hidden costs include the fees on your **401(k),** which can equal more than 30 percent of your money over a lifetime. Recent laws make companies disclose the costs associated with 401(k)s, but still the real costs may not be fully revealed. Here are some additional hidden costs and fees in retirement plans the investor should be aware of:

- Trading Costs
- Brokerage Commissions
- SEC 28(e) Soft Dollar
- Sub-Transfer Agent Fees
- Account Distribution Fees (Sales) Based 12(b)-1

It is crucial to ask your advisors if they charge for any of these fees; most do! Have the advisor disclose all fees and costs of any plan you are considering.

Inflation:

Let us discuss **inflation** and how it works. You must plan for it even though you may not see it, because it is there.

> *"A nickel ain't worth a dime anymore."*
>
> – YOGI BERRA

> *"Invest in inflation. It's the only thing going up."*
>
> – WILL ROGERS

Generally, inflation is caused by a money supply that expands too rapidly, or money is too easy and there are not enough goods being produced.

Here are some examples of inflation:

- In 1965, a car cost $1,600; in 2015, $30,000.
- In 1965, a home cost $21,500; in 2015, $350,000
- In 1965, a gallon of gas cost $0.31; in 2015, $2.78.

Average Annual Inflation
by decade

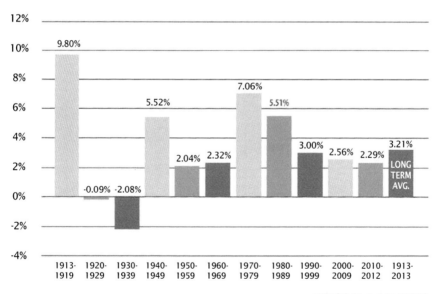

©2013 InflationData.com. Updated 4/15/2013

* Inflation is a silent but a deadly drain of finances, and it can erode real returns in a way that may be unnoticeable. It can truly affect your buying power by making your money less valuable.

Keeping up with inflation is sometimes done by investing in securities products that help fight inflation. By only investing in safe returns such as CDs or bank instruments, an investor is actually losing money by not even keeping up with inflation. This simply means that the interest rate you earn is less than the rate of inflation. Current rates are so low that you are actually losing money after you factor in taxes and inflation on fixed instruments such as certificates of deposit and money markets, savings and checking accounts.

Understand that the effects of inflation need to be addressed by you and your advisor or it will significantly impact your retirement without anyone ever knowing it happened.

Taxes:

Taxes are one of the most important considerations when investing for retirement.

There is no one who cares for taxes, and taxes are such a significant part of planning for retirement both during and after retirement that everyone should know how to benefit from the tax code. Yet many fall short when it comes to tax planning in retirement.

Knowing which plan type will benefit you the most is vital to the success of your plan's performance; consulting with the right tax advisor or especially financial advisor, who is knowledgeable, is invaluable to your overall success.

Not only can the proper advisor help direct you on which plan to choose but also which plan might be the best to maximize tax write-offs and/or tax credits. Making sure you end up with more money before, during and after retirement is the ultimate goal. Remember, the rich loathe taxes, and so should you, when it comes to your money!

"I'm proud of paying taxes. Only thing is I could

be just as proud for half the money."

— ARTHUR GODFREY

Types of Taxes:

- Ordinary Income Taxes
- Estate Taxes
- Probate Taxes
- State Taxes
- Federal Taxes
- Capital Gains Taxes

I have to study tax-law changes as they relate to the advice I give my clients concerning their retirement. Taxes have become a large part of my practice, specifically knowing the ways to reduce or eliminate taxes when possible. Therefore, my best recommendation is to find a knowledgeable advisor who discusses taxes and investing, and not just the latter.

Taxes on Social Security Income

Many retirees may not know there is a hidden tax when you retire. Yes, each individual is taxed on his or her Social Security income, so you need to beware of this before you elect to take your Social Security benefits.

Retirees are paying taxes as high as 85 percent of their Social Security benefits. Prior to 1983, Social Security was tax-free! Then, in 1983, Congress legislated that up to 50 percent of your Social Security benefits could be taxed when your combined threshold income exceeded certain thresholds. Then, in 1993, the law was amended, and now it allows up to 85 percent of your Social Security benefits to be taxed.

The IRS calculates the tax on your Social Security benefits based on your provisional income from all sources including pensions (IRA and 401[k]), income and municipal bond funds. Your interest earned from mutual funds, brokerage accounts, CDs, tax-free bonds, and savings are all added together.

What Is Provisional Income?

Pension Income

\+ Interest Income

\+ Tax-Exempt Benefits

\+ 50% of Your SS Benefits

= *Provisional Income*

If your provisional income is between (married filing jointly):

$0-$32,00 No SS tax is imposed

$32,000-$44,000 Up to 50% of your SS benefits are taxed

$44,000 & Up Up to 85% of your SS benefits are taxed

— SOURCE: SSA, SSA Pub. Number 05-10024, February 2002

Tax Levels:

- **Single:** Income of $25,000 up to $34,000, 50 percent of excess above $25,000 is taxable, not to exceed $4,500.

- **Single:** Income over $34,000, 85 percent of excess above $34,000 is taxable; it cannot exceed 85 percent of amount received from Social Security.

- **Married:** Income of $32,000 up to $44,000, 50 percent of excess above $32,000 is taxable, not to exceed $6,000.

- **Married:** Income over $44,000, 85 percent of excess above $44,000 is taxable; it cannot exceed 85 percent of amount received from Social Security.

Knowing Your Tax Bracket is important:

2014 Taxable Income Brackets & Rates

RATE	SINGLE FILERS	MARRIED JOINT FILERS	HEAD OF HOUSEHOLD FILERS
10%	$0-$9,075	$0-$18,150	0-$12,950
15%	$9,076-$36,900	$18,151-$73,800	$12,951-$49,400
25%	$36,901-$89,350	$73,801-$148,850	$49,401-$127,550
28%	$89,351-$186,350	$148,851-$226,850	$127,551-$206,600
33%	$186,351-$405,100	$226,851-$405,100	$206,601-$405,100
35%	$405,101-$406,750	$405,101-$457,600	$405,101-$432,200
39.6%	$406,751+	$467,601+	$432,201+

You need to know what your taxable income is and what tax rate you are charged on your income. Most clients with whom I sit down do not know this.

Go to Line 37 of lasts year's tax return. The AGI, or Adjusted Gross Income, is the amount on which you pay income taxes.

Reducing Social Security Taxes

The taxes on Social Security income is not that complex. For example, if you make over a certain amount of money — $25,000, $32,000 or $44,000 — then you are taxed on that amount of Social Security income at either 50 percent or 85 percent.

What's even simpler, if you can reduce the amount of taxable income you receive from other sources (anything for which you get a 1099) and get below that certain amount of income, you can reduce Social Security taxes!

Here are a few ways to reduce your Social Security taxes:

- Convert your IRA to a Roth IRA, so you do not have to take RMDs (required minimum distributions.) These RMDs can reduce your taxes significantly if you can afford to convert and do not need that income.
- If you qualify for life insurance, buy that with any taxable money you

are just going to transfer and leave to your beneficiaries anyway.

• Use tax-deferred annuities to transfer any taxable investments — CDs, money markets, stocks, bonds and others that you receive a 1099 on and that you want to defer the taxes on.

• Use a reverse mortgage for income as the income, you receive is not taxable since it is a loan.

• Use a loan or second mortgage to supplement income, as any loan is not taxable.

This tax was originally designed with good intentions. It was designed to tax the rich who were collecting sizable pensions and other income while also receiving Social Security income. However, like everything else, it ended up hurting the middle class more than anyone.

The chart on Page 47 is a worksheet so that you can to calculate your own taxes on your Social Security income.

Another hidden cost results from not being able to discuss or communicate effectively with your advisor about your money. This simply means you need to understand what you are both trying to say to each other, especially if you do not understand what the advisor is talking about. Do not just nod your head in agreement when you do not know what is being said. Tell the advisor, "I don't understand that," or "Can you break it down in laymen's terms so I understand it more clearly?"

Simply ask your advisor to speak in dollars and cents and not in percentages or terms you may not understand. Ask them what that amounts to in dollars per year. Tell your advisor to explain it to you as if you are a third-grader.

For example: An investor may have a $1 million brokerage account with a 1 percent fee per quarter. It may not sound like much, but let's do the math: 1 percent per quarter is $2,500, so in four quarters, that is $10,000. Now that is not much when you are making money and the market is going up, but do not forget that you pay that same amount when the market goes down, as well. Being aware of these fees and costs is ultimately how you can reduce or eliminate them. Also, everything is negotiable. If your advisor tells you that their fees are not, then find a new advisor.

Taxation of Social Security Benefits

A portion of Social Security benefits may be subject to income taxation.
The following worksheet will assist in determining that tax.

1. Social Security benefits for the year $ _____

2. 50% of line 1 _____

3. Modified adjusted gross income:
   a. AGI less net Social Security benefits received _____
   b. Tax-exempt interest and dividends received or accrued _____
   c. Line 3a plus line 3b _____

4. Provisional income (line 2 plus line 3c) _____

5. Applicable "first-tier" threshold[1] _____

6. Line 4 less line 5 (not less than zero) _____

7. 50% of line 6 _____

8. Amount of benefits subject to tax (smaller of line 2 or line 7) _____

If the "provisional income" (line 4, above) does not exceed the corresponding "first-tier threshold) line 5, above), no amount is taxable. However, if provisional income exceeds the corresponding threshold, continue with the worksheet below.

9. Applicable second-tier threshold[1] $ _____

10. Line 4 minus line 9 (if less than zero, enter zero) _____

11. 85% of line 10 _____

12. Amount taxable under first-tier (from line 8, above) _____

13. Applicable dollar amount[1] _____

14. Smaller of line 12 or line 14 _____

15. Line 11 plus line 14 _____

16. 85% of line 1 _____

17. Amount of benefits subject to tax (smaller of line 15 or line 16) _____

FILING STATUS	FIRST-TIER THRESHOLD (FOR LINE 5)	SECOND-TIER THRESHOLD (FOR LINE 9)	APPLICABLE $ AMOUNT (FOR LINE 13)
Married filing jointly	$32,000	$44,000	$6,000
Married filing separately (but lived together part of the year)	$0	$0	$0
All others	$25,000	$34,0000	$4,500

NOTE: This is not an official IRS worksheet. CAUTION: Any increase in income, such as from the sale of a stock or a retirement plan distribution, may subject you to an unexpected tax on the Social Security benefits.
[1] See applicable table in column.

The biggest cost to you is the cost of not being educated or adequately informed when it comes to your money!

Other Fees and Costs to Consider:

- Banking
- Credit Cards
- Travel
- Auto, Home and Health Insurance
- Long Term Care
- Life Insurance
- Mutual Funds
- Variable Annuities (one of the highest-fee products)

Some people say, **"If you don't understand something, then do not buy it!"** In my opinion that is the stupidest statement I have ever heard! Almost everything in this life is unknown or misunderstood. For example, do you understand how your television, cell phone, microwave, or any other complicated device works? Yet the average person uses these on a daily basis and really does not know how they really work. This is the same with most financial products that people buy and own. Ultimately, investors do not understand everything about the investment products they purchase, and they just use them as recommended by their advisors, if the products make sense to the investor.

Generally, most people do not know how their mutual funds, IRAs, 401(k)s or other investments really work. But it is possible to learn and educate yourself with the right advisor helping. In fact, many of the advisors selling and offering these financial products are unaware of how they work or how the fees are really structured. Just ask your advisor what the "real" costs are! Prepare for some stammering and stuttering.

We live in a **debt-driven society,** and many of the fees and costs will continue for our entire lives, like it or not. You will always be in debt. Even if you are wealthy, there will always be bills, costs, or fees because we live in a society where all goods and services have costs. Money makes the world go round, so to speak.

Although your house is paid off, there are still bills, taxes, insurance, repairs, and maintenance fees, and it never ends. Just realize that success with money depends on how you deal with reducing and eliminating these costs. These are mainly fees, taxes and inflation.

I would like to discuss **"free"** or **"no cost,"** which does not really mean "free." A perfect example of this is your IRA, 401(k) or pension plan. Just because there's no cost does not mean you do not pay fees. All investments of any kind have fees and costs; you may not be aware of these costs, but they are there, hidden or otherwise. The saying "no free lunch" means there is a hidden cost, even if it says "free."

Mutual Fund Fees:
- Expense-Ratio Fees
- Transaction Costs
- Tax Costs
- Cash Drag
- Soft Dollar Cost
- Advisory Fees

All of these fees and expenses are in the prospectus that your broker or advisor gave you, so it's up to you to read it. It is impossible to estimate how much your investment with a securities product actually costs you. Your money is divided in so many different ways on Wall Street that it is an unknown cost that I believe cannot be accounted for. Every time a stock, bond or commodity is bought or sold, there is a cost on that security, and ultimately the investor pays that cost, even if unaware.

If your money is not in your house under your mattress, then you are paying costs or fees, hidden or not. If it is in your house under your mattress, then you are losing money to inflation.

In conclusion, costs — mainly fees, inflation and taxes — never end. Reducing these costs can help you manage your mistakes, which will be explored in our next chapter.

4

MISTAKES

Mistake: *an error in action, calculation, opinion, or judgment caused by poor reasoning, carelessness, insufficient knowledge, and so forth.*

This all reverts back to education. With proper education, mistakes can be limited, reduced and avoided that ultimately save you money on your retirement.

> *"Anyone who has never made a mistake has*
>
> *never tried anything new."*
>
> — ALBERT EINSTEIN

Mistakes are going to happen because they are part of life and most definitely a part of investing for retirement planning. However, the fewer mistakes you make the more money you will have, so it makes sense to make as few mistakes as possible. Your education can be in direct correlation to the success or failure that results with your investing or retirement plans.

> *"The more you know the fewer mistakes you*
>
> *will make! The fewer mistakes you make with*
>
> *your money the more money you will retain or*
>
> *accumulate!"*
>
> — JOSEPH THOMAS

We have already discussed how not conversing about your money can be a problem and a mistake especially when it comes to your significant other. Make sure to discuss and communicate about what you think you should be doing with the money that both of you control.

I have labeled this mistake the **spousal mistake** because men and women are usually significantly different on investing and risk tolerance, and most often men and women have opposite beliefs about the risk they should take with investing. It is crucial to understand each other's views, and many marriages end up in divorce over money. Couples need to understand their own different views before investing.

My experience has proven that men are usually the breadwinners and will always take more chances with investing. Also, men are more willing to gamble with investing and see what happens, whereas women are just the opposite; they will be satisfied with a safe return as long as they do not lose money. I believe this is because of the way men and women's brains are wired. You need to know what the other person is thinking before you invest.

You also need to know your spouse's view of retirement, as many empty-nesters end up in divorce because of retirement when they both failed to plan for what they both wanted individually as well as a couple. Having one spouse handling the finances can also be another mistake. As we know, problems happen and both partners need to be prepared for the future especially when married.

Another key to a successful retirement plan that can limit your mistakes may be to **live within or below your means.** You may want to downsize from that large house where five people used to live and now there are only two.

Sometimes the mini-van may not be needed anymore; you may even want to get by with one car. You may want to look at things much differently than you used to. Making the right purchase decisions in retirement can help avoid mistakes.

Being realistic when talking about money is also very important, as many people never want to talk about the mistakes they have made or the money they lost. These war stories are generally kept very quiet, and most people tend to only talk about how wonderfully they have done, when in fact it is not true. Being realistic with yourself, your spouse and your advisor is imperative to your success. Many people have lost and will lose money in the stock market. No one wants to admit how foolish they were when instead they would rather tell you how smart they were.

In brief, do not go through life with rose-colored glasses, but instead see things for what they really are and be realistic about your money — which in turn can help you see more clearly.

Having an advisor who's too optimistic can be another mistake. I happen to be one of the most optimistic people around, but when it comes to advising clients about their money and how to protect their money, I am somewhat pessimistic. I tend to prepare and structure my clients' accounts with a certain degree of safety so that if investments go wrong, my clients are well protected.

The worst scenario is an advisor or broker with an **"everything is wonderful attitude."** You need to know the upside and the downside of your investments, which means looking at the good and bad of what can happen to your money in both good and bad times.

I have seen many clients who come to me after a previous advisor told them **not to worry** about their investments losing value. As soon as your advisor says those words, it is time for a second opinion or maybe even a new advisor because you need to have someone who will be open to change when change is needed.

If the market starts dropping and you feel threatened, get out and regroup. Do not listen to your advisor who has no economic ties to your money telling you not to worry about it. That is the last thing you should be hearing. If you have concerns, it is usually for good reason.

Next, I want to discuss diversification, because most advisors really do not know what diversification means. Most investors do not know, either. It can be a huge mistake to not truly diversify your money when it comes to retirement planning.

Diversifying means to spread your investments into different types of investments, with **different levels of risk.** This way if one investment does poorly or loses value, you still have another investment that will be there and will not lose. It is critical to spread your risk between the investments you choose to buy or own in your retirement plan.

The chart below simply shows the correlation between risk versus reward tradeoff. This relates to the return on the type of investment "risk" you choose.

Risk/Return Tradeoff

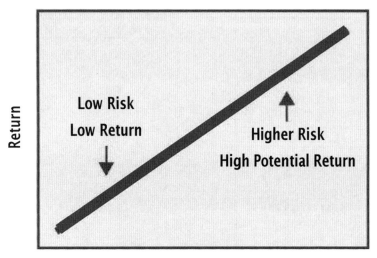

Standard Deviation (or Risk)

The higher the risk, the more the reward. The lower risk, the lower the reward. That is why a combination of both makes better investment sense.

We also talked about **advisor diversification** so that different advisors may manage different portions of your money, and this spreads out risk — which therefore diversifies your investments even further. Unfortunately, most advisors recommend you put all your eggs in one basket. You may not even know it.

Meanwhile, you have heard the saying, **"Never put all your eggs in one basket!"** Why do you think this saying has been around as long as it has? Because it is true, and people have learned it to be sound advice!

"Yet most recommendations advisors and brokers make are <u>dead wrong</u> when it comes to diversification."

Some advisors may discuss diversification, but in reality they will have all your money at risk all the time, or they will tell you that they will put a percentage of your money in bonds for safety. That is basically the same level of risk in many respects, because you can still lose principal in bonds just as you can in stocks. For example, if you have a brokerage account and you have mutual funds and stocks, then your money is at risk at all times. That is not diversification, because your money is at risk in similar risk-level investments and both can lose significant principal.

Mutual funds fluctuate, and so do stocks, so they are at risk all the time. Therefore, you have the same risk level. Even though they are different investments types, the level of risk has not changed.

Understanding that the main reason your advisor has made certain investment decisions over others is because that is what they get paid to do. If you are at a bakery, you will most likely be buying baked goods. If you go to a stock broker, you will be buying stocks. Too many people make wrong assumptions about why certain advisors did not offer other types of products. The reason is because they do not sell other products. So just make sure to identify what the advisor can and cannot sell!

You must understand that <u>true diversification</u> means spreading your risk by having different levels of risk and safe investments that cannot lose value when others do.

Having different advisors can further diversify your money, as we have already discussed. <u>This is why you may want different advisors handling different investments for you so you are further diversified, and then you have some investments that do not lose money when others do.</u>

I see many people walk into my office and want me to review their brokerage statements. These clients are in their 70s or 80s, and **100 percent** of their money is invested in stocks or mutual funds.

All of their money is at risk all of the time if the market has a significant correction. This is not diversification.

I label it **gambling,** and as I have said before, some know they are gambling with their retirement and others do not. I want you to know either way. I explain they have no diversification, and they tell me they do. Why? Simply because the advisor told them so.

Investing requires taking some risk, but many people take too much risk. As I have previously mentioned, some know they are risking or gambling with their retirement, and others do not. Just realize that higher returns means higher risk. Some investors believe they are immune from losses and others think they will sell at the right time if they need to. Unfortunately, no one can really time the market so the importance of managing and limiting risk is vital to an investor's success.

This is specifically why so many people lost billions of dollars during the most recent crash — the housing crisis — because **no one explained to them that stocks, bonds, mutual funds, or any other securities products lose value even if you have different types. They are all risky investments.** _**The risk level is the same**_**; it is high risk.** Investors can lose money if the market goes down.

Let me put this in perspective. There is nothing wrong with risk or having mutual funds, stocks and bonds in a portfolio, but what is wrong is that most advisors do not know how to diversify a client's assets by having less risky investments that cannot lose value. That is the problem. This may be because your advisor only sells risky investments and cannot offer safer alternatives.

Furthermore, what happens if you need your money or die at the wrong time when the market is in a correction? Or what happens if you have retired after 30 years, and on the day you moved his 401(k), the market went down 30 percent or 40 percent or more?

There are alternatives that can be in place to prevent total devastation of this client's retirement account, but the advisor did not advise the client of this. It is criminal.

The reason why you need to spread your money out into many different investment vehicles, with different levels of risk and safety, is so this does not happen to you during the next correction.

Here is a great analogy I heard on a radio program: If you were going to have your bathroom and your roof fixed because they both needed repairs, would you have the same person repair them both?

You call your local plumber to fix your bathroom. He brings in his shiny toolbox, and there is only one tool in it — a big red wrench. He says, "I'm here to fix your bathroom." Would you let him in? Most likely!

You tell him about your roof, and he says he can fix that also: "No problem." He says he has the tool to fix that, as well, and it's the same big red wrench. Would you let him fix your roof and your bathroom? No!

Unfortunately, that is exactly what advisors do every day, and most investors do not know any better or realize it is happening to them. The client needs to ask and be educated about true diversification.

In summary, **you need different investment tools to accomplish different goals for your money**. In addition, you may need to have different advisors because that way you can spread your risk even further from losses.

You need to know the purpose of your money and then pick the right investment vehicle for that money. Also, determine what risk level you want for that specific money.

One tool for every job is not a good idea, and it's not sound financial advice when it comes to your retirement money. Having both safe and risky investments percentages prevents losses and protects your money from devastation when in bad times. This is common-sense investing — or at least it should be.

Many advisors and investors today just do not think about this in real terms. There are people like Suze Orman on CNBC and other so called financial gurus telling people the only method is to invest all your money in the stock market no matter what the circumstances.

This just is not fair to the people who do not know any better.

An advisor's age and experience is another criteria you may use when considering an advisor and determining your risk levels for diversification.

For example, if you are 65 years old and your advisor is 35, in most cases you are going to be advised as a 35-year-old would invest. Most advisors do not invest your money as a 65-year-old would but rather they invest money as a 35- year-old would. They generally invest your money in risky or riskier investment choices, because they have the time to recoup losses. You do not! Also, they may not understand why risk diversification is needed at age 60, 70 or 80 more than any other age. Your age should determine your risk tolerance and your diversification levels based on your specific age.

If you are 65 years old, then 65 percent of your money should be invested in safe investments and 35 percent should be invested in riskier investments. Keep in mind; this depends on many factors which I will explain later in this chapter.

Definition of Risk Tolerance:

The degree of variability in investment returns that an individual is willing to withstand. An individual should have a realistic understanding of his or her ability and willingness to stomach large swings in the value of his or her investments. Both your age and your timeframe for meeting your specific goals play a role in determining your risk tolerance.

When you are younger and have a long time to meet your goals, you may have a higher risk tolerance than someone who is nearing retirement and is counting on income for the rest of his or her life. Other factors such as personality, personal experiences with the market and current financial circumstances also come into play with the risk levels you choose. These choices vary from client to client.

Some clients cannot tolerate risk. I have seen so many clients who tell me they want out of the stock market and want something with **zero risk** because they cannot sleep at night or get physically ill when they think about the thought of being broke and losing all their savings. No matter what your advisor may tell you about how this cannot happen, if you are diversified do not listen to him or her. If your intuition tells you to sell, then sell.

If you want safer investments, find safer advisors who offer safer investment alternatives.

You may not think this happens, but it does every day. You just do not hear about it. I have been told by many clients how they or another person have lost it all in risky investments simply because of bad advice from good advisors. It is imperative to understand that too much risk is not for every investor.

There are **safe alternatives** with less risk that your advisor or other advisors can offer you; however, they may not, because they do not make as much commission as some of the other products they sell. Or worse, the advisor may not be able to offer you these safe products because their company will not allow it. Therefore, it is your job to seek out other advisors that do offer safe product types as a percentage of your portfolio.

"Most people are more concerned about the RETURN ON their money. But I am more concerned about the RETURN OF my money."

— WILL ROGERS

Here are some safe alternatives you may want to consider when diversifying your portfolio for safety:

- Government Bonds
- U.S. Treasury Notes
- Certificates of Deposits
- Bank Instruments FDIC
- Annuities (fixed, indexed and immediate)

All of these products are designed to provide safety and levels of risk that are minimal as compared to securities.

Risk tolerance does not mean what percentage of stocks and what percentage of bonds you own! It needs to be based on your acceptance of risk and safety at the same time. You need both risk and safety in your portfolio.

<u>Age versus Risk Allocations and Percentages:</u>

As an advisor, I am so tired of hearing the same old allocation advice from the so-called "financial experts" telling everyone as a whole to have a 60/40 or 50/50 stocks and bonds portfolio to lower investment risk. Nothing can be further from the truth, as both of these products are 100 percent at risk all the time. Instead they need to distribute their assets in different categories of risk and safety.

The following allocations and diversification percentages are based on age, and this is what I advise my clients to use when planning for their retirement.

True Diversification Based on Age:

Investment choices should be invested in the level of risk tolerance that makes you feel comfortable in each category based on your age.

<u>*As you will note, nothing has changed investment wise, just the percentage of allocation has changed based on your age.*</u>

Age 30

30% Safe: Government Bonds, Certificates of Deposits, Annuities: Fixed or Indexed, Savings, Life Insurance, Gold and Silver.

70% Risk: Securities: Stocks, Corporate Bonds, Mutual Funds, Commercial Real Estate, EFTs, REITs, Commodities and other Security Products.

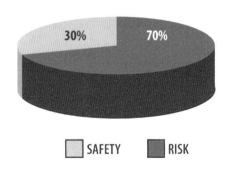

Age 40

40% Safe: Government Bonds, Certificates of Deposits, Annuities: Fixed or Indexed, Savings, Life Insurance, Gold and Silver.

60% Risk: Securities: Stocks, Corporate Bonds, Mutual Funds, Commercial Real Estate, EFTs, REITs, Commodities and other Security Products.

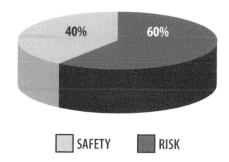

Age 50

50% Safe: Government Bonds, Certificates of Deposits, Annuities: Fixed or Indexed, Savings, Life Insurance, Gold and Silver.

50% Risk: Securities: Stocks, Corporate Bonds, Mutual Funds, Commercial Real Estate, EFTs, REITs, Commodities and other Security Products.

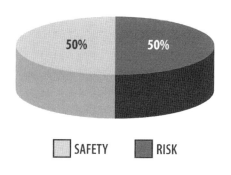

Age 60

60% Safe: Government Bonds, Certificates of Deposits, Annuities: Fixed or Indexed, Savings, Life Insurance, Gold and Silver.

40% Risk: Securities: Stocks, Corporate Bonds, Mutual Funds, Commercial Real Estate, EFTs, REITs, Commodities and other Security Products.

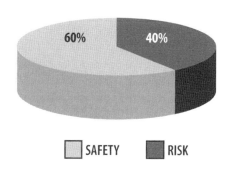

Age 70

70% Safe: Government Bonds, Certificates of Deposits, Annuities Fixed or Indexed, Savings, Life Insurance.

30% Risk: Securities: Stocks, Corporate Bonds, Mutual Funds, Commercial Real Estate, EFTs, REITs, Commodities and other Security Products.

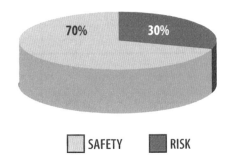

Age 80

80% Safe: Government Bonds, Certificates of Deposits, Annuities: Fixed or Indexed, Savings, Life Insurance, Gold and Silver.

20% Risk: Securities: Stocks, Corporate Bonds, Mutual Funds, Commercial Real Estate, EFTs, REITs, Commodities and other Security Products.

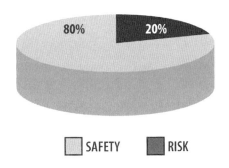

As an investor and depending on other criteria, it may be wise to change these allocations based on your own specific needs and tolerance. For example, if you have the wherewithal to withstand significant loses and you are not worried about losing principal, then by all means you may want to increase the percentages until they favor your position. Maybe you will never need this money, and you want to gamble with it. Perhaps it is going to be left to older children who already have money. Whatever the situation calls for, it is up to you what risk levels you choose.

My recommendation is that *your age should equal the level of safety you should have in your portfolio.*

Investors should understand that protecting their money the older you get is imperative and having an advisor who also understands this may be priceless.

When you are younger, it is possible to take more risks with your money. When you are older, this is not the case. You do not have the time to recoup the losses.

Selecting the correct advisor who understands these concepts is extremely important for you, the investor, because you are the one with your money at risk and not your naïve advisor. Let's make that very clear: **it is your money at risk and not the advisor's.** Your advisor has nothing to lose. You do.

Additional Mistakes You May Make:
- Not educating yourself continually.
- Picking the wrong advisor for the job at hand.
- Selecting the wrong investments.
- Choosing the wrong way to diversify.
- Picking the wrong people to listen too.
- Choosing the wrong safety level you need.
- Selecting the wrong tools to use for retirement.
- Not knowing your downside on every investment.
- Not taking advantage of the tax code when investing.
- Not being open-minded to change when necessary.

Mistakes To Avoid with Your IRA or 401(k):
- Failing to update and change beneficiaries.
- Keeping your 401(k) at your previous job.
- Thinking your "will" covers your IRA or 401(k).
- Not splitting your IRA into different beneficiaries.

- Naming your trust as your beneficiary.
- Not using the stretch IRA privilege.
- Thinking your company will help you.
- Failing to rollover your IRA within 60 days.
- Thinking your banker, broker, brother-in-law or someone else will help you with your money. Remember the burden is on you and no one else.

Investing in what you know:

If you are going to buy stocks or any investment, buy companies with which you are familiar and do business with every day, such as Coke, Home Depot, McDonald's, Apple, and Exxon. Or buy mutual funds that have big-name companies you know or with which you do business as a part of the portfolio. This will give you a level of comfort, knowing they are visible and known worldwide. One of my wealthiest clients told me about this strategy while I was on his yacht in Florida.

Generally, the bigger the company, the less failure rate there will be. Some people may mention Enron, but that is another book I would need to write to explain. For now, just accept the fact that you should invest in companies you know, that are highly visible and with which you do business regularly.

This is important if you are going to buy stocks, bonds, mutual funds, securities or other financial products, as well. Especially when buying insurance products, bigger is generally better, and bigger means safer.

There are also no **get-rich-quick schemes** that ever worked, and that is why people were easily duped by Bernie Madoff and their greed. There are no shortcuts in retirement planning. This is your nest egg, and you need to look long term 10 to 40 years ahead. Some people have a hard time thinking that far down the road, but you need to plan even if you cannot see the end of the road.

Choosing the **type of plan** you want for your money is imperative to your success, and planning for the good and the bad will limit your mistakes.

Selecting the right type of plan, such as a **government plan** (qualified plans) versus **your plan** (non-qualified plans), can mean the difference in many taxes versus no taxes or fewer taxes. You need to decide which you prefer for your retirement. Also, decide what combination is right for your success. Selecting the right advisor or knowing which plan is best for you can make a huge difference in your success. Maybe a combination of both may make sense for you, the investor.

Tax rates have increased with the Affordable Health Care Act (Obamacare), and if you do not plan, then these mistakes will come back to haunt you and your family for a lifetime! You need to know how you or your family will be taxed now and in the future and plan for those possible changes. My point is that even though this act was all about health-care reform, the government slipped in areas of taxation. That is something that can affect your income if you are unaware.

Beginning in 2013, a 3.8 percent Medicare surcharge took effect on investment income (including dividends and capital gains) for income above $200,000 for individuals or $250,000 for married couples filing jointly.

Taxes rates are increasing for many, and the government will continue to nip and tuck the tax code. You need to adjust your planning with those considerations in mind. You need to search for advisors who have the latest tax-advantaged products or concepts and legal remedies that can be used to continually reduce or eliminate taxes as the rich do. It is for your benefit.

Let us talk about **buying low and selling high.** Everyone who has ever bought any stock knows this saying, but very few ever do what they know to be the case. Most investors wait until the market or stock is going up and then they buy. When the price goes up, they wait too long to sell. Unfortunately, they buy at the high price and sell at the low price, which is just the opposite of what they should have done.

Most people get **stock tips** from a friend or someone they know who generally has no idea how good or bad the stock is. Then they buy based on a simple recommendation without one bit of research. Also, people do not consider how good the company may or may not be. Sometimes, it is like the blind leading the blind. They think together they will succeed. Wrong! I have had many clients tell me their barber, window washer or Realtor told them to buy this stock or that stock, and nine out of 10 times, they lose money and wonder why. It is because the people giving the stock tips generally have little or no knowledge. This is free advice, so take it for what it is worth. And free advice goes past stock tips — sometimes, bad tips will lead you to the wrong advisor. Remember that Bernie Madoff came highly recommended.

Let's talk about interest rates and using certificates of deposits as investments. Most CD investors did well in years past when rates were much higher, but lately rates are so low you owe the bank money. Rates have tumbled because of recent economic conditions and the Fed lowering interest rates. The government will continue keeping rates low to keep the economy going, and the government wants you to invest in the stock market so that the economy performs better. Many CD investors know the risk is too high investing in the stock market; therefore, they are waiting for interest rates to go up.

This is the mistake of **being too safe** with your money and not changing when you need to seek out alternatives for your money like the rich do. Unfortunately, these people are waiting for someone else to tell them to do something different. This is clearly the mistake of not taking some risk to increase your rates of return. If you put all your money in very-low-risk investments, then you are giving up an enormous opportunity over a lifetime.

These safe-return investors have faith and trust in the banks they deal with, and most are waiting for things to change. Once they do change, these investors believe that the bank will surely tell them what to do with their money. Unfortunately, nothing could be further from the truth. The bank wants to pay you low interest so they can loan your money out to others at higher rates for car loans, mortgages, credit cards and personal loans.

People are not realistic when it comes to the economy. The Federal Reserve has said it will not significantly raise interest rates for years to come, yet every day someone tells me rates are going to go up. It does not make sense. These people need to wake up and smell the coffee. Look around and realize things are changing.

Success has to do with being willing to change when it is warranted. There are safe alternatives to CDs such as fixed annuities or bonds; however, you need to be willing to change habits.

Choosing the wrong pension option:

Another mistake people make after they retire from a company is that they are given choices about which payment option they should choose when it comes to their pensions. Many people make major mistakes here that can cost their spouses and their families the entire pension if the wrong option is chosen. Making sure you seek out the advice of an advisor who is knowledgeable in this area is priceless.

Pension maximization is using life insurance in a way to gain needed death-benefit protection while offering you an opportunity to maximize your defined-pension benefits. In other words, you choose the maximum benefit offered by your pension and take the difference you would have given up and buy life insurance to cover the loss of pension benefit for your spouse.

For example, let's say your maximum benefit is $1,000 per month if you take a full pension; however, you leave nothing for your spouse if you die. Your spouse would prefer you choose the option that leaves them 75 percent of your benefit, or $750 per month if you die. The difference is $250 per month, so take the $1,000 and use the $250 difference to buy life insurance to cover you in the event of your death so you do not disinherit your spouse.

Being worried or fearful is another key mistake people make. For example, some people are too scared to do anything, so they simply keep their money where it is so they feel comfortable. To the contrary, they need to move their money to meet the surrounding conditions whatever they may be.

The **old dog, new tricks concept** comes in to play here. With some people, it is impossible to show them new ideas or ways to invest their money even if it is the best investment in the world. You cannot convince these type of investors; more specifically safe-only investors. They are waiting for interest rates to come back when in fact they are losing money every day. Instead they could invest in something just as safe but they cannot convince themselves to do so. This means you need to be open minded as an investor and accept change and look for the current product that may help you until the situation does change.

Mistakes you need to look out for:

Listening to the wrong people or the know-it-alls:

We talked about taking advice from the wrong people earlier in the book, but I want to reinforce that it simply means to think about from whom you are receiving financial advice. Just because they are related to you, or they work at a bank or are actually an advisor in some capacity does not mean you will take their advice and act on it. You will take in the information, interpret it and decide if that advice fits your needs or solves your problem at hand, then move forward.

Not understanding tax consequences of IRAs:

Understanding that any qualified retirement plan such as your IRA, 401(k) or pension all come with taxes and this means you will be taxed if you take out lump sums. Not being aware of this means you may be taxed excessively with the wrong advice. I have heard people tell me that their brother-in-law told them to take their IRA and cash it out and pay off their mortgage, not knowing that they had just incurred a huge tax bill. This advice was absolutely criminal, but people do it every day unaware of the tax consequences, because someone who you thought knew more than you recommended it.

Not understanding that Social Security is taxed:

Many people retire and start taking their Social Security benefits unaware that the income is taxable depending on your income. Also, you need to be aware that the tax rates start at 50 percent up to as high as 85 percent.

Not withdrawing your IRA's RMD after age 70.5:

This one is very critical, so do not get caught by the IRS with this one. If you do, you'd better beg for forgiveness. If you do not take the **required minimum distribution (RMD)** set by the IRS once you are age 70 and 6 months of age you will be penalized 50 percent of what you were supposed to take out, so if your RMD was $10,000, you can be penalized $5,000. Make sure you understand this one!

The chart on page 69 is a worksheet to calculate your own RMDs.

Required Minimum Distributions
Calculation Worksheet:

ADD ALL:

IRA balances on December 31 of previous year   _____

Distribution period from Uniform Lifetime Table   _____

IRA balance *divided by* distribution period = RMD   _____

Uniform Lifetime Table

For use by unmarried retirement account owners, married owners whose spouses are not more than 10 years younger, and married owners who spouses are not the sole beneficiaries of their IRAs.

Data taken from 2013 Table III in *IRS Publication 590 (2012), Individual Retirement Arrangements (IRAs)*.

AGE	RMD	AGE	RMD	AGE	RMD
70	27.4	80	18.7	90	11.4
71	26.5	81	17.9	91	10.8
72	25.6	82	17.1	92	10.2
73	24.7	83	16.3	93	9.6
74	23.8	84	15.5	94	9.1
75	22.9	85	14.8	95	8.6
76	22.0	86	14.1	96	8.1
77	21.2	87	13.4	97	7.6
78	20.3	88	12.7	98	7.1
79	19.5	89	12.0	99	6.7

Getting caught by the 20 percent withholding penalty:

This is another one of those areas that happens to people because they listen to the "know-it-alls" out there.

If you are going to move your pension plan, 401(k) or other company retirement plan, make sure you know that you may have 20 percent withheld for taxes because you chose to do it yourself without having an asset-to-asset transfer. You have the check sent to yourself instead of the company that will accept your money. Doing this, you will now have the IRS take out 20 percent of all your funds, and you will be taxed on the 20 percent. So make sure you have someone who knows about rollover pension options before electing to do this one yourself.

Owning assets the wrong way:

How you title your assets is extremely important, and I am not getting into how you should title your assets. Just know that you need to see an attorney who can help you plan for the proper way so that you can avoid taxes and other problems that can crop up after someone passes away without properly titled assets.

Not reviewing your insurance plans:

Realize that all of your insurance plans, mainly life, health, long-term care and Medicare supplement insurance, will be a big part of your life once you are retired. Reviewing these plans is as imperative as reviewing your investment accounts.

Not planning year after year:

Remember that retirement and retirement planning is not "set it and forget it." Reviewing your accounts, plans and goals is an ongoing ritual that needs to be addressed and maintained as often as you feel comfortable. I do not recommend anything less than every year. Things change rapidly today, and you need to be updated.

Planning for your money to last a lifetime:

To reduce these mistakes we have just covered and others we may not have discussed, as a general rule seek out the true professional who can help with your specific problem at hand. For example, see an attorney for the legal issues; see the accountant for the tax issues, and see the specialist for the needed advice you seek. More importantly, do not take advice from others who may want to help but only hinder you with their incompetence, lack of experience and lack of credentials. Beware of the know-it-alls.

The solutions for many of these mistakes are obvious, though they are not always easy to implement. They boil down to education, discipline and managing your emotions in most cases. Simply being aware of these mistakes can help significantly.

This leads us to the next chapter about the types of **retirement plans** you may want to use.

5

RETIREMENT PLANS

Retirement Plans: *IRA, 401(k), TSA, 403(b), 412(e), Pensions, Simple IRA, Roth IRA, SEP, 457 and ESOP. There may be others, but these are the most commonly used.*

> *"The tax laws were written for business owners*
>
> *and investors."*
>
> — ROBERT KIYOSAKI, *RICH DAD, POOR DAD*

I believe that all of the tax laws were written for the advantage of the rich and well-informed.

Qualified Retirement Plan: A plan that meets the requirements of the Internal Revenue Service tax code and, as a result, is eligible to receive certain tax benefits. The one thing that all of these retirement plans have in common is that taxes are deferred for a later date and the plans are "qualified" by the IRS. In order for your retirement plan to be qualified, it must be an approved IRS plan: IRA, 401(k), Roth, or any other qualified plan type and these qualified plans come with tax benefits, tax consequences and rules to follow.

Non-Qualified: A plan that does not meet the requirements in the pertinent provisions of the applicable regulations, as for tax or pension plan considerations. A non-qualified plan means it is not a qualified retirement plan IRS-wise, and it has its own rules regarding taxes.

The investor will not get the write-offs tax-wise and may not have to follow certain rules as the qualified plans must, but they can still be used for retirement. These plans can be securities, annuities, life insurance, mutual funds or any other investment.

Qualified plans are all about taxes because you are deferring or putting off your taxes until you need the money to live on, and then, you are taxed. Tax deferral helps your money grow faster simply because you are not being taxed on your money until you need it. Even though all IRA plan types are tax deferred and this eventually means you will be taxed, this is not as bad as you think. Tax deferring is a good thing, and this is how you are able to accumulate money much faster as compared to taxable investments.

Retirement plan benefits:
- You initially get the write-off on your income taxes, thus reducing your income level and tax bracket.
- You are earning interest on your principal.
- You earn interest on your interest.
- You earn interest on the money that would have been taxed if you had it in a taxable account.

Here is a quick example of how after-tax yields work when comparing tax deferred versus taxable:

If you were to receive interest in the amount of 5 percent per year that is tax deferred and you are in a 28 percent tax bracket, you would have to earn 6.94 percent in a taxable account. In addition, you also had the write-off on your taxes. As you can see, the benefits are substantial.

Why compounding of interest works well with IRAs:

If $1 was invested and it doubled every year for 20 years, at the end of 20 years with taxes of 28 percent taken off, you would have $51,353.37.

If you invested that same dollar over 20 years with taxes deferred, you would have $754,974.72.

Now that is the power of tax deferral! Tax deferral makes a huge difference.

See the chart on Page 75.

Taxable Equivalent Yields

The following chart enables you to determine the yield required from a taxable savings plan to match that of a **"tax deferred"** savings plan. Read **down** the first column to find the tax deferred interest rate and **across** the top row for your approximate tax bracket.

The taxable equivalent yield is found where the **tax-deferred row** and the **tax bracket column** meet.

INTEREST RATE	INCOME TAX BRACKETS				
	15%	25%	28%	33%	35%
3.00%	3.53%	4.00%	4.17%	4.48%	4.61%
3.50%	4.12%	4.67%	4.86%	5.23%	5.38%
4.00%	4.70%	5.33%	5.56%	5.97%	6.15%
4.50%	5.29%	5.99%	6.25%	6.72%	6.92%
5.00%	5.88%	6.67%	6.94%	7.47%	7.69%
5.50%	6.47%	7.33%	7.64%	8.21%	8.46%
6.00%	7.06%	7.99%	8.33%	8.96%	9.23%
6.50%	7.65%	8.67%	9.03%	9.71%	10.00%
7.00%	8.24%	9.33%	9.72%	10.45%	10.77%
7.50%	8.82%	9.99%	10.42%	11.20%	11.54%
8.00%	9.41%	10.66%	11.11%	11.94%	12.31%
8.50%	9.99%	11.33%	11.81%	12.69%	13.06%
9.00%	10.59%	11.99%	12.50%	13.44%	13.85%
9.50%	11.18%	12.66%	13.20%	14.18%	14.62%
10.00%	11.76%	13.33%	13.89%	14.93%	15.38%

"The greatest mathematical discovery of all time."

— ALBERT EINSTEIN'S REFERENCE TO COMPOUNDING INTEREST

The longer you can defer taxes, the more money you will have period.

Compounding is the process of generating earnings on an asset's reinvested earnings. When you combine tax deferral and compounding of interest, you have a winning combination.

I will use the word **IRA** as a synonymous term for all qualified retirement plan types: IRAs, Roth, 401(k), etc.; they are all generally taxed the same way. The only thing that generally changes is the contribution limits and eligibility requirements.

What is an IRA?

Let me start by explaining that an IRA is simply an account that can shelter your retirement in order to help you save on taxes during your working years. You can open an account at an investment firm, insurance company or bank.

You can fund your IRA with any type of investment you want, such as stocks, bonds, mutual funds, securities, annuities, real estate, gold, certificates of deposit, money markets or any other IRS-approved investment vehicle.

You receive a tax write-off on the contribution you make, and this, in turn, reduces your income taxes. The write-off amount depends on the type of IRA plan you choose. If you are a business or high-wage earner or you work for a corporation, the contribution limits will vary and can be substantially higher than that of an individual IRA.

For example, if you are an owner/operator of a business, you may open an SEP (simplified employee pension) plan, and if you work for a corporation, you will most likely have a 401(k). The point is that they all have different uses and contribution limits, but all are deferring your taxes until you take the money later as retirement income.

Keep in mind that the **contribution limits** are going to change from year to year, and generally, they will increase each year so that you can contribute more money. If you are age 50 or older, there are catch-up provisions that allow you to contribute extra money before you retire, and these amounts vary from plan to plan. These amounts also change and usually increase year to year.

See the chart on Page 77 which shows the plan type and contribution limit based on your individual income eligibility.

IRA[4]

IRA contribution (Under age 50)	$5,500
IRA contribution (50 & older)	$6,500
IRA deduction phase-out (qualified plan participant)	
Single or HOH	$60,000-$70,000
Married, filing jointly	$96,000-$116,000
Married, filing separately	$0-$10,000
Spousal IRA deduction phase-out	$181,000-$191,000

PHASE-OUT OF ROTH IRA CONTRIBUTION ELIGIBILITY[4]

Single or HOH	$114,000-$129,000
Married, filing jointly	$181,000-$191,000
Married, filing separately	$0-$10,000

SEP[4,11,12]

SEP contribution	Up to 25% of compensation (limit $52,000)	Employer contribution	Up to 25% of compensation
Minimum compensation for SEP participant	$550	Employer salary deferral (under 50)	$17,500

SIMPLE[4]

		Employer salary deferral (50 & older)	$23,000
SIMPLE elective deferral (under age 50)	$12,000		
SIMPLE elective deferral (50 & older)	$14,500	SIMPLE elective deferral (50 & older)	$52,000 ($57,500 age 50 & older

OTHER RETIREMENT PLANS

401(k), 403(b), 5 governmental 457(b), and SARSEP elective deferral (under age 50)	$17,500
401(k), 403(b), 5 governmental 457(b), and SARSEP elective deferral (50 & older)	$23,000
Limit on additions to defined contribution plans	$52,000
Annual benefit limit on defined benefit plans	$210,000
Highly compensated employee makes	$115,000
Maximum compensation taken into account for qualified plans	$260,000

Clients ask me all the time, which plan is better, a **traditional IRA** or a **Roth IRA.** It usually depends on your goals and whether or not you need the write-off tax wise. However, I would recommend the Roth IRA because of the tax benefits, as it is not taxable. My opinion is that tax free outweighs taxable every time.

Some key points to ensure that you get the most from your IRA are to make sure you contribute the maximum allowed each year and not only have an IRA but also a 401(k) or additional plan, if your tax advisor agrees.

You are allowed to have more than one kind of IRA. It depends on your income tax status and how you may get paid, and also if your spouse has a plan or does not have a plan. Check with your tax advisor regarding this.

Additional points to understand with IRAs:
- Start required minimum distributions at age 70.5.
- Withdrawals are taxed.
- All transfers should be asset-to-asset transfers.
- Change your beneficiaries as needed.
- Change your investment choices as needed.

Common questions on IRAs:
- What is the Required Minimum Distribution amount?
- Can I combine more than one IRA with another IRA?
- Can I combine my IRA and my 401(k) as one account?
- Should I convert my IRA or 401(k) to a Roth IRA?
- Can I leave more to my heirs by converting to a Roth IRA?
- Should I use the Stretch IRA laws on my IRA?
- Should my children or my grandchildren be my beneficiaries?
- Can I reduce the taxes on my IRA distributions?
- Can I own an IRA and a Roth IRA?
- How can I eliminate annual fees from my current IRA?

IRS-approved Qualified Plans:

- IRA
- 401(k)
- Roth IRA
- Roth 401(k)
- 457
- 412
- Pension
- SEP
- Simple IRA
- SAR SEP
- Self-Directed IRA
- Annuities: *(can be qualified or non-qualified)*

Each one of the above plans is basically the same in that you can reduce your taxes by contributing, and later on, you will be taxed when you take income. Each plan has different contribution limits, but ultimately they are all taxed the same — as ordinary income.

As we have already discussed, tax deferred means eventually you will pay taxes on the distributions you must take out at age 70.5. You, your spouse or named beneficiaries will pay taxes as well unless it is a Roth IRA. You can convert your IRA/401(k) to a Roth IRA, and then you are no longer taxed.

There are both pros and cons to an IRA-Roth IRA conversion, and in my opinion, most people should convert to a Roth IRA because of the tax benefits. If you think tax rates are going down, then do not worry about converting to a Roth; however, if you think tax rates are going up, then a conversion is a good idea.

Note that the IRS will allow an IRA-Roth IRA conversion after your death if your spouse thinks that will benefit him or her. You can also revert back to a traditional IRA if you converted to a Roth and prefer to change back.

Let's discuss this right now: You will pay the same amount of taxes on your IRAs whether or not you convert to a Roth IRA. However, you might pay fewer taxes now because if tax rates go up, then you will pay more; it is that simple. Consider converting from an IRA to a Roth IRA because it is a discount tax-wise, especially if you feel tax rates are going up in the future.

With qualified IRA money, the earliest you can take money out without a penalty is age 59.5. If you withdraw money before age 59.5, then you will incur an early withdrawal penalty. It would be in the amount of 10 percent of the amount you take out, plus you are then taxed as ordinary income taxes on that amount, as well.

There are ways to take money out of your IRA before age 59.5 if you use the **72-T laws.** You can avoid the 10 percent pre-59.5 penalty if you take lump sums or monthly income of 5 equal distributions or longer or over a life period.

Annuities are a great tool to use for this because of their income distribution features. You can use an annuity to accomplish this as long as a five-year or more equal distribution is met.

In my opinion, the plan type or investment vehicle you invest in is not as important as the goals you want to reach for that specific money you have earmarked with a specific goal. For example, you may want to earmark who or where this money is going to end up: children, wife, family, charity or others. Be sure it gets there in the most tax-advantaged ways possible.

If your goal is to leave money to your family tax free, then a Roth IRA or life insurance is most definitely the most tax-advantaged way to go, and the investment that you earn interest on is secondary.

When I am discussing different types of plans or investments, many times I have clients ask me for something new, investment-wise or retirement-wise. I usually respond by asking, what would that be?

You see there are really only a few categories of investment types out there in the real world of investments.

Investment categories for retirement plans:

Securities: High Risk

- Stocks, bonds, mutual funds, futures/commodities, stock options, REITs, and others.
- All are subject to risk and can lose principal.

Property: Moderate Risk

- Real estate: residential and commercial investment and speculative.
- These are subject to market fluctuation and can lose value.

Guaranteed Accounts: Low Risk

- CDs, savings, money markets, annuities, life insurance, and U.S. government bonds

- All are safe and cannot lose principal.

Four general categories of investments:

Cash:

- Products you buy from a bank, insurance company or government agency.

- These are safe instruments that generally cannot lose value.

Bonds:

- Products you buy that may be issued by a corporation,
- Government or Municipality. Generally stable but can lose value.

Stocks:

- Products that you buy as a shareholder or that you buy from a securities firm. May include gold and silver as well.
- All are at-risk investments and can lose value.

Property:

- Real estate that you buy in the form of both residential and commercial property investments.
- Generally stable but subject to loss.

There are hybrids of many of these categories and there may be products that have different labels than these 4 categories, but most investments end up in these areas.

It all comes down to investment risk, and the real question becomes, **"How much risk do you want or can you afford?"** You can be invested in anyone of the four of these categories and still have a qualified retirement plan.

You can also have a self-directed IRA that only invests in real estate or gold or whatever investment you want, as long as it is qualified and meets IRS guidelines. Any one of these investments can be your investment vehicle for your retirement plan.

Knowing what each risk level means is extremely important. Also, being aware of how much risk you are willing to take will determine in which categories you will invest and your allocation in those investments.

Let us discuss taxes a little further and how to take advantage of the tax codes that are on the books. Most likely these laws will be "grandfathered" if the laws change. This means that if the laws change in the future and you already made the transaction, then most likely they will not go back and tax you if you already made the transaction.

Again, this all comes down to what the wealthy in this country have known for years. Becoming wealthy has nothing to do with how much money you make or earn, but it has to do with how much money you keep and save without being taxed.

The 3 biggest tax breaks:

Roth IRA:

It is 100 percent tax free while you live and while you take out withdrawals; it has no required distributions, and you can pass it to your heirs 100 percent tax free as a death benefit. What is wrong with this? Nothing!

Stretch IRA:

It allows you to pass your IRA to a younger family member (named beneficiary) and allows them to delay taxes or defer taxes for many years.

As a result, you can increase the amount of money in your IRA by not having to pay it out immediately upon your death. Therefore, you can leverage your money significantly.

To go a step further, you should consider having the Roth IRA and using it with the Stretch IRA provisions. Now you can maximize your IRA and leave significant amounts of money 100 percent tax free!

Life Insurance:

Using life insurance is the same as using any other investment tool. You need to see this for what it really is; there are no magic bullets here, just dollars and cents.

Simply look at using life insurance as a way of buying future dollars at a discount. If you want to leave your heirs 100 percent tax-free dollars, then life insurance is simply the best way to go. In fact, there is no better solution available in the estate-, financial- and/or retirement-planning world than the use of life insurance.

Use your required minimum distributions to a higher level so instead of just reinvesting this money and being taxed all over again, buy life insurance and then you are leveraging your money. Another choice is to take all or some portion of your IRA and purchase life insurance. Generally, you will leave your family a 2-to-1 value as compared to the IRA by itself. It is actually more, because you are leaving your family 100 percent tax-free dollars instead of 100 percent taxed dollars. This can save an additional 39.5 percent or more in ordinary income taxes depending on the size of your estate.

> *"If a man doesn't believe in life insurance, let him*
>
> *die once without it. That will teach him a lesson!"*
>
> — WILL ROGERS

Malcolm Forbes, in the Los Angeles Times on Dec. 12, 1989, stated that much of his company's income is being used to purchase "enormous sums of life insurance," a device that can legally transfer millions of dollars in cash to his beneficiaries without an estate tax assessment.

Ask yourself this question when considering what assets you may be leaving to your heirs:

What would you rather leave your heirs to inherit?

A. $1,000,000 IRA (invested in whatever you want)

B. $1,000,000 annuity (any type there is)

C. $1,000,000 life insurance policy

D. $1,000,000 Roth IRA

The clear answer is C and D simply because they are 100 percent tax free. Why do people think life insurance and Roth IRAs are so bad? They may not be educated enough to make this decision or they have been told by the know-it-alls that this is a bad idea. The key to this question is that it does not matter what the investment is; the tax liability is most important when passing assets. Where your money ends up and how it is taxed, in my opinion, is significantly more important than the rate of interest you earn. Ask your advisor: What is more important, earnings or taxes?

Another hot topic today is **annuities,** and there are so many moving parts to an annuity that I can tell you it is virtually impossible for you to know all the ins and outs of any annuity!

In the state of Florida and most other states, new laws were enacted regarding annuities in an effort to protect the senior population during the purchase of annuities — and rightfully so. For the average person, annuities are so very confusing, whether you are buying them or even just reviewing the contract you already own!

Annuities are legal instruments written by attorneys and interpreted by attorneys, and in general, they legally favor the insurance companies.

After many years of seeing clients who purchased annuities from other agents no longer in the business, I can tell you that it usually starts with a phone call, and then the client shows me the existing contract.

They usually say something such as: "What do you think about this one?" after they throw three inches of legal paperwork on the table with a thud. Invariably, I ask them, "Do you understand and know what you bought?" Then, I start by asking questions to see if they will ever use this annuity for what the annuity was intended, which is income. You see, most clients never even use the annuity for the purpose they originally intended. An annuity is geared for future income.

I become very concerned when clients explain to me how they think their existing annuity works and what their agent (who is no longer in the business) told them about how their annuity works. They believe their annuity is the best thing since sliced bread. I am here to declare that in most cases, there is nothing further from the truth! The annuity does what the contract says it will do — nothing more and nothing less.

By the way, each and every annuity contract is different and unique, and each one does something different. All annuities are not created equal! This is why I am uncovering the truth behind any annuity that you own, want to own, or want to know about, as it relates to you and your specific needs as an annuity consumer!

The Basics:

I do not need to explain who Clint Eastwood is, but I will remind you of one of his most enduring roles in the famous Sergio Leone "spaghetti westerns" that made him a household name: "The Good, The Bad and The Ugly." If you can remember that movie, you will be halfway to understanding which annuity may be right for you.

The Good
- <u>**Any annuity that fits your specific needs!**</u>
- Fixed
- Indexed
- Immediate

The Bad

- <u>**Any annuity that does not fit your specific needs!**</u>
- Variable Annuities

The Ugly

- <u>**An annuity that can be too complicated!**</u>
- Hybrid-Type Annuities

Let us go in-depth, to provide you some insight into my professional opinion on certain annuities that you may want to avoid. If you already own one, getting rid of it might be your best option, depending on your specific needs.

The Bad

I have been licensed to sell variable annuities since 1982, when there were only three companies offering them. I thought they were a very good product for younger people who were maxed out on their 401(k) or IRA, and needed an extra vehicle to defer taxes. These products were designed for younger consumers and not for seniors, and I still believe that today.

Unfortunately, the variable annuity companies have been losing sales over the past 10 to 15 years, because of all the attention to the success of index annuities. So, the insurance companies reinvented the wheel with variable annuities. They now worked like a fixed-index annuity and an immediate annuity all rolled up into one, except for one "bad" thing: the product is still a variable annuity with all the fees and charges they had before, but with bells and whistles the average senior probably will not ever use.

I can continue here about variable annuities, but I will instead give you some reasons why they are classified as **the bad.** I believe other annuities can accomplish the same thing as variable annuities without the fees, and without risking 100 percent of your principal at all times!

Fees, Fees and More Fees: Variable annuities are notorious for fees, and this is where you should start, no matter what the annuity you are buying or already purchased. How do you pay for your annuity? Through fees!

According to the investment research firm Morningstar, the average expense is 2.44 percent with a variable annuity, but on average, I have found it's actually anywhere from 2.5 percent to as high as 4.5 percent. For example, a $100,000 variable annuity may cost anywhere from $2,500 to $4,500 per year each and every year for as long as you own it. Worse, even if your account is losing money, they still charge you those fees. What kind of investment charges you a fee even when you are losing money? Variable annuities do!

There are many extras sold with variable annuities, but my opinion, and that of many other experts, is that the death benefit rider is the worst of all, and I will explain why.

The **death benefit rider** basically gives you a death benefit based on your account's highest value it had reached, and is locked in if you die. Sounds good, right? Wrong! There are several very important reasons; first being you have to die, so someone else gets your money. Not that great a proposition, if you ask me. Who wants to die in order to free up the money in a variable annuity? No one! You want your investments to grow and make money while you live. This is not a product you want to be stuck with in life or death.

LIMRA, an insurance-industry research group, found that less than 1 percent of variable annuity policies paid a death benefit from 2002 to 2004. If you want a death benefit, then buy life insurance and do not buy variable annuities for a death benefit.

Here is how it works: If you die and leave the variable annuity to your beneficiaries, it is all taxable at the beneficiaries' tax bracket anyway. If you bought life insurance, it's generally 100 percent tax free. And you don't pay annual fees for a death. Makes sense, right? Yes! This is not rocket science; it is money, and it needs to make sense.

I cannot believe how many senior citizens who are very savvy, frugal, and smart with their money are conned into buying something they know nothing about and even the agents themselves do not understand. It is astonishing!

A very interesting point about variable annuities is that all are sold by stock brokers who sell stock and securities. If stock brokers are so good at recommending stocks and securities, why are they selling you variable annuities?

Maybe because the commissions are more than selling stock! Ask any stock broker about index, fixed or immediate annuities, and they will tell you how terrible a product they are. Simply because they are not allowed to sell them, please consider this the next time a stockbroker offers you a variable annuity.

The big picture is that you must know what you are buying; if not, do not buy it. Before I go any further, I must let you know that it is impossible for me or anyone else to explain everything you need to know about annuities in their entirety. The only way to come close is by defining your financial suitability and needs as a starting point, and then finding the product that best fits those needs.

We already talked about second opinions, and this is imperative with annuities. Most clients ask their friends, their neighbors, and anyone who they think can help them with their annuity purchase. This is a good practice but does not even come close to what you should be doing when it comes to researching the purchase of an annuity, especially a variable annuity.

Rule Number 1:

Always get a second opinion from a second source! Do not ask the person who sold you the annuity in the first place if it is a good annuity; ask an annuity advisor.

Rule Number 2:

Find out if you should replace your old annuity. Every insurance company and agent gets paid when you purchase a new product, so of course they will always have a new deal, better than the one you own now. Generally, a new contract will benefit you, but not always. If you have an older annuity paying you a fixed guaranteed rate of, say, 3 percent or higher, it may not benefit you to move it to a new product, because rates have come down.

The 1035 Exchange, the replacement, switching, or upgrading to a new annuity may not be in your best interest every time, so ask how and why this will benefit you immediately, as well as in the long run.

New "surrender periods" lock you up for years to come, and you may have limited access to your money, so be aware that there are what I call velvet handcuffs that come with a new contract.

Rule number 3:

Annuities come with velvet handcuffs. Remember, if you are buying any annuity, they all come with a large number and variety of rules. **The most important thing to know is how those rules affect your ability to access your money when you need it.** You also need to know how they function, and you especially need to pay attention to these terms: surrender charges, penalty-free amounts, annual fees, rider fees, when you can take payments and for how long, how the death benefit works, and many others.

The Good

I am not going into great detail on these annuities; I am just going to preface myself by saying that these are the better types of annuities for a larger cross-section of retirees and seniors that will fit many of their needs. However, they can be just as complicated as variable annuities, but with lower annual fees. More importantly, your principal is protected and not exposed to market risk as it is with variable annuities.

Index annuities may also be confusing and complicated but offer many benefits over other annuities for the right investor. Again, you need to know what velvet handcuffs you'll be wearing with the product and for how long. It just depends on your specifics.

Suitability is the key here. Your circumstances must be suitable to purchase an index annuity, and it must meet your needs in regards to when you need to access your money, and how you can access money.

The Annuity Basics: Definitions

Annuity: An annuity can be defined as a contract which provides an income stream in return for an initial payment.

Immediate Annuity: An instrument that allows a person to convert a sum of money into a guaranteed series of payments for a period equal to the greater of the person's life or a certain number of years.

Deferred Annuity: A deferred annuity contract allows you to accumulate tax-deferred earnings during the term of the contract, and sometimes add assets to your contract over time. Your deferred annuity earnings may be either fixed or variable, depending on the way your money is invested.

Fixed Annuity: A type of annuity that provides payment of a specific sum of money at a fixed rate of return for a fixed period of time. In addition to guaranteeing your principal, a fixed rate annuity earns a guaranteed rate of interest for a specified period of time. Very close to Certificate of Deposit issued by a bank.

Fixed-Index or Equity-Index Annuity: An annuity whose earnings are tied to the performance of a market index or indexes (i.e. the Standard & Poor's 500®). fixed index annuities are intended for the "accumulation phase" of retirement savings.

The Ugly

There are many hybrids of all annuities, and each one may do different things to accomplish goals as an investor, but for the most part I recommend my clients stay away from the most complex annuity contracts _unless you completely understand how they work or what they will do for you._

It is amazing how much bad press surrounds annuities, when in fact nothing can be further from the truth. Annuities should be and are used by smart investors to protect their assets, keep up with inflation and guarantee their income like no other investment available today!

Annuities provide something called **triple compounding of interest** because they are tax-deferred vehicles. This is how triple compounding works:

- Interest on your principal
- Interest on your interest you earned
- Interest on the taxes you would have paid

The biggest disadvantage to annuities is surrender charges, and if you understand that all annuities have them, you will be able to make an educated decision as to how long you will own this annuity. You see, the sooner the surrender charge disappears, the sooner you can access all your money without any fees for cashing it in.

Annuity Points:

- Annuities have **no probate taxes** because they have a directed named beneficiary, which means you save anywhere from 3 percent to 10 percent in probate taxes.

- Annuities have **creditor protection** because they have a named beneficiary and insurance policies are generally not attachable in law suits.

- Annuities are **incontestable** which means, no one can claim they were your long lost cousin who wants half of your money. You choose the people you want to leave the money to and no one can challenge it.

- IRAs and annuities are generally **lawsuit proof** in most cases.

I use annuities in many cases for many of the reasons I mentioned above, but even though they are tax deferred, which is a good thing for taxes, it is a bad thing when you leave this to your heirs. Proper planning needs to be discussed regarding their use in your retirement plan.

One of the biggest and most advantageous benefits of annuities that no other financial product can do is to guarantee your income for the rest of your life.

Many of my clients buy annuities for the safety of principal they provide, the fixed interest rates that are generally higher than the bank, the accessibility of income or lump sums without fee, the fact that you can pass assets to a loved one as a joint owner with zero taxes and so many other features of certain specific contracts.

Next let us talk about using **different types of trusts** for the benefit of taxes and protecting one's assets including retirement money.

Charitable Reminder Trusts

A CRT allows you to donate any asset to a named charity and receive certain tax benefits and tax favored income.

The old adage of "you need to give to receive" certainly applies with CRTs. I have worked with many clients in this area, and I can tell you that they are some of the most beneficial tax codes there are that favor the donor (you), so make sure you look into them or find an advisor who knows how they work.

Irrevocable Life Insurance Trust

What most people may not realize is that depending on the size of your estate, life insurance can be taxable depending on ownership, so the ILIT makes sure that you can leave all of your life insurance to your beneficiaries' tax free.

Private Charitable Foundation

This is another way to be philanthropic while receiving big tax breaks. You can set up your own charity or family foundation with your name on it and if you follow the rules, you can basically perform miracles tax wise. Many of the richest families in the world have set up family foundations for tax reasons, the legacy of their names and income in the most tax advantaged ways possible.

Blind Trusts

One of the best ways to hide your money or prevent people from finding out where your money is or invested in is a blind trust. You basically put your assets in the trust, and a third party has total control of your money. There are certain other benefits to investing and asset protection as well.

Private Retirement Trust

It protects wealth and assets inside the trust. Even if you are being sued, you still may be able to put assets in the trust to prevent them from being attached while being sued while in litigation. This is great for protection of assets you do not want anyone to access.

The plans discussed in this chapter are some of the best ways an investor planning for retirement may want to implement, but without a **"plan of action,"** it may be a moot point therefore the next chapter will discuss how to put a plan of action into place for retirement.

6

PLAN OF ACTION

Plan of Action: *an organized program of measures to be taken in order to achieve a goal.*

"By failing to prepare, you are preparing to fail."

— BENJAMIN FRANKLIN

It is crucial to have a "plan of action" — or, at a minimum, write an outline of your requirements for what your specific retirement looks like. You need to plan so you can succeed because otherwise procrastinating never results in reaching your goals. A Fortune magazine article from 1999 said that investors who have written plans end up with five times more money as compared to those who do not. This is reason enough to have a plan.

How To Implement a Plan of Action:
- Write it down.
- Number-crunch everything.
- Set your goals and "name your money." Label it.
- Separate long-term versus short-term goals.
- Be realistic with time and returns.
- Always make dollars and cents of investing.
- Leave emotions aside.
- Pluses are better than losses.
- Know your level of risk.
- Diversify using real diversification.

A few quick points here should include **getting organized** and knowing where all your money is at all times. Also be aware of how your money is performing, and for how long, and who benefits from it if you die. If you choose to, let your loved ones know where and what you have as far as investments are concerned.

When setting financial goals, you may want to look at what you have done in the past to help you make the right decisions now and in the future. Find your motivation to get this done; if it means making or saving more money, whatever helps you succeed, just do it.

Setting **realistic goals** is also important; they cannot be so unreasonable that you may never reach your goals. Take baby steps and move forward each time if you need to, but just keep moving forward. Set dates for accomplishing certain goals and try to adhere to those dates if possible.

Remove bad choices from your repertoire, meaning you cannot fall back into your old habits. Make every financial decision count in the best possible way.

Tracking your progress is also another task to do on a regular basis. Some of my clients do not track any of their money or gains, and this can lead to disaster if you are not careful. You need to know where, what and how your money is doing at all times.

Get help when you need it. This means seeking out advisors who may be able to help you with their specialized knowledge. Or, you can make sure you spend time learning about the aspects with which you need help. Solve issues and problems as quickly as they arrive by finding the right advisor that fits your needs.

Know what retirement planning means:

In the simplest sense, retirement planning is the planning you do to be prepared for life after paid work ends, not just financially but in all aspects of life. The nonfinancial aspects include such lifestyle choices as how to spend time in retirement, where to live, when to completely quit working, and so forth.

Retirement is the point when you stop working completely. <u>My definition:</u> <u>You work hard while younger so you can stop working when you are older</u> <u>and have enough money to do so.</u>

Define your own retirement as you see it:

Cultivate some ideas of how and what your retirement will look like. This is the point at which you need to write down your objectives, listing your most important goals first. It helps to be very specific about what you want to accomplish. Also be ready to change and adapt as warranted by surroundings.

Take account of all your assets:

Account for all your assets, including the ones you may not think of every day, like antiques, classic cars, jewelry, hobbies that could make you money, your second home or real estate that may turn into income or cash later on if needed.

Evaluate your health now and in the future as needed:

Enjoying the rest of your life in retirement is important, and making sure you keep physically and mentally fit is more important. Annual physicals may be in order, and commit to eating properly and exercising so you can enjoy your years in retirement.

Keep busy:

Many retirees need to realize that retirement does not mean to do nothing, as keeping busy can be one of your best assets. I have found that most of my clients, who have a social life, join organizations and give back to the community by volunteering, have a much better outlook on life than those who do not.

Determine when you want Social Security to start:

There is much debate on whether or not to start your Social Security income. My opinion is that if you need the money to live on, then start the payout. Otherwise, if you are going to have to pay taxes on the income deposit it in the bank and be taxed, then do not take it.

Realize that Social Security benefits are taxed depending on income. Some of my clients have found ways to reduce or eliminate these taxes. Many people retire without realizing that Social Security income is a taxable income; it is not tax free.

Decide if you want to work through retirement:

Unless you are financially independent, you will most likely want to work in some capacity for as long as you can or need to. This may be one of your goals as to whether or not you want or have to work during retirement. It is going to depend on how much income you have accumulated and if you will be able to sustain that income for the rest of your life. Also, keep in mind that you may be taxed on this income, and it may increase your tax bracket, so all of these considerations need to be addressed. Tax brackets for retirement may also not be as low as you have been led to believe. There has been misinformation about tax rates. Once you retire your tax bracket will be lower, but this has been proven to be untrue. Many times retirees have higher rates than when they were working, simply because they now have several income sources instead of just one.

Create a realistic budget:

You need to know how much money will be coming in, how much debt will be incurred and how to reach your goals. You will need to track your income and expenses over a six-month period prior to retiring and figure out if you will have enough income to support your current lifestyle or not. If not, you will have to make changes as needed.

I advise my clients who are about to retire that it will take at least one full year before they know how they are doing, money-wise and tax-wise. This is because your lifestyle may change and you will find that you may need more or less income than you originally thought, but either way you will not know for a while.

Find ways to cut expenses:

You may want to start thinking about what bills you can reduce or eliminate when you are retired, so paying off your house or car may be something you should decide to do.

Eliminating expenses from your daily life that are frivolous may warrant consideration. We all have different things we can or cannot live without, and determining them can help in planning your retirement.

Plan for the unknown or unexpected:

None of us know what is going to happen, so planning for the unknown is one way to help prepare us for emergencies. You need to consider a side fund for the unexpected repairs or costs that appear in life such as: car repairs, roof leaks, dental bills or other expenses that crop up when least expected. I recommend six months' worth of income to be set aside in an accessible account such as a money market.

Stick to your plan:

This step can be difficult, but it is rewarding to know that you persevered and found the determination to keep on the right path even when times got tough.

Make sure your plan of action can be changed according to outside factors such as: the economy, changing technology, inflation, your age and your needs. Ask yourself, "Do I need more income?" Do you want to loan money to your family or do something else that will affect your money? As a result, you must consider changing your plan as needed.

Understanding that your plan of action is not set it and forget it. **You must be willing to adapt.** Clients tell me about investments they or a family member bought that are now worthless because they never changed or adapted to outside factors. It really helps to see what is going on around you. I cannot tell you how many clients I meet who wait until the last minute to make investment decisions that affect their money, when instead they should have acted sooner rather than later.

For example, stock market trading is done by high-speed computers that make up approximately 50 percent to 70 percent of all trades on Wall Street. Obviously, the computer has no emotions and does not care about how good or bad the company will do in the coming years; all it does is compute whether or not to make a trade based on a profit. The profit can be a penny, and it makes millions of trades to make profit, so when people tell me that their money is safe in the market, I just shake my head in disbelief realizing they have an unrealistic view of the investment world.

As I have said before, "No one will ever understand how Wall Street works," so it is important to just keep it simple. Realize investing in the stock market is not the only choice. Therefore, you need to search out alternative products which can give you a certain level of safety with potential growth designed for your specific money you are willing to invest as a percentage.

Furthermore, people fake what they know sometimes. For instance, I have clients who pretend to understand or are informed, but in reality they are just pretending because they do not want to look ignorant. Never do this; remember to just ask and that no question is a stupid question. Asking questions is how we learn.

Generally speaking, it is impossible for the average client to understand all of the complexities of the investments that are sold since there is just too much legal jargon that surrounds them. Therefore, all you can do is to educate yourself with an advisor who wants to teach you and spend time with you in order to understand how a product can help you personally. Success happens by taking your time to reach educated decisions and using research that is available to you.

Understand what this product does for you and how it helps reach your investment goals for that specific money invested. Just remember to understand the basics as they apply to you and your money.

Also, you must realize you will never understand everything, because that is impossible. No one is a know-it-all with everything in life, especially retirement planning. The success level for you as an investor is so dependent on what you know and what you do not know that I cannot emphasize this enough.

Keeping control of your money is also very important! **Never give up your control of your money.** Too many people do not know what trades are being made with their money by their brokers at the brokerage house and to give up too much control means you have too much to lose.

I had a client in North Carolina who told me that his broker had made more than 190 trades in one year on his wife's $10,000 IRA. This again is just criminal. There is no reason for this other than the broker was trying to churn the account to make more commission.

Labeling your money is also something you want to get into the habit of doing when investing. This way, you know the purpose of the specific amount of money you are investing. Ask yourself, is it short term or long term? What is the purpose of this money — savings, emergency, retirement, beach house, new car or other uses? By labeling it, you will understand more clearly how you can invest it and what the risk level should be.

Identifying the amount or the percentage, what specific asset to use, and for what purpose can help you select what investment level of risk you will choose. In addition, you may choose who this money is going to and that may also set the stage for the risk level. For example, you may want 100 percent of your IRAs to be invested aggressively in a mutual fund, and you may leave this money to your spouse if you pass away. If this money is going to purchase a car in three months, then most likely you will only keep this in your checking account, but if this money was labeled "college funds" then you may be willing to invest for a number of years. You need to know what the purpose of your money is.

Purpose for Money:
- Pay Off Home
- Retirement Income
- Retire at Certain Age
- No Debt
- College for Children or Grandchildren
- Pay Off Debt
- Start Family Business
- For the Children
- Money in the Bank
- Tax Free
- Taxed Later

Steps to take to prepare a plan of action:

Run Calculations:

Crunch the numbers annually, so this way you know your financial position at least once per year at a minimum. Running numbers and reviewing your returns can also help you determine if you are going to invest more or close the account and move on.

Decide to invest more for retirement:

This goes for whether you are retired or planning for retirement. You need to learn to continually save money and put it away for a later date. This does not mean *not* spending money. Think about ways to make money with your money when it is not being spent.

Decide when you will need income:

This may be one of the most important aspects of retirement planning. So many retirees put off, wait too long or just think they can do without, and it is truly the key to success for many retirees.

When do you need income, it is a question that you should be asking yourself as often as you need to. Also, do you want interest from your investments to pay you? Or do you want to spend down your money over the rest of your life or a period of time?

Are your current income streams sufficient enough to live on and pay your daily bills? Knowing this is vital. I cannot stress this enough. Realize that you need to know when you need income to start. Too many people wait too long or live under their means when they do not have to do so.

Knowing how long your money will last becomes imperative to the retiree. I have many clients who would prefer to do without when instead they could make life much easier on themselves. Some want to make sure they never run out of money; others were Great Depression-era people who were taught to be frugal just to survive; others simply do without so they can make sure their families get whatever they do not spend. If it were up to me, more people would make it easier on themselves and start their income streams sooner rather than later, and enjoy the rest of their lives.

Continue to educate yourself:

Remember that education is so important because as human beings we are constantly learning. That means you need to continue to educate yourself before, during, and after retirement, especially with changing times.

Have annual reviews with your advisors:

Let us face it, things change, and you need to be aware of these changes. For example, tax laws are always being changed. Health care for the elderly is under attack by Washington, and you need to know how this may affect your money and retirement, so it is critical to have an annual review with your key advisors. Remember getting a second opinion from another advisor is something you may also want to incorporate with your annual reviews.

Organize and combine older retirement plans:

Your IRA and your 401(k) are literally the same type of retirement account tax-wise, so you can combine them if you would like. Many retirees as they get older just find it difficult to keep up with all the statements and different investment accounts they have, so in order to make it easier for yourself, combine accounts that are similar.

This also makes it easy for your partner, spouse or family members to know where all of your money is when you do pass away. Often there are billions in unclaimed funds because people die and their loved ones do not know all the accounts they owned. Unfortunately, they go unclaimed.

Review your health-care benefits and costs:

Knowing what you will pay for your health care after retirement is so important; many people do not understand that it can be such a large part of your income once you do retire.

For example, I recently had a client who worked for 37 years at a job. His pension income was $1,400 per month; however, his health insurance was $1,700 per month. Realize you need to plan for these costs.

Prepare for long-term care needs:

Another area of health-care costs is long-term care insurance. Many people today have found out with parents or relatives being in a nursing home that it can cost you your entire life savings in a few short years with no planning or insurance.

Unfortunately, we have all heard the war stories of people who had to give up all their assets to a state-run facility in order to qualify for the nursing home and then died shortly after and all those assets were lost. This is simply because they did not plan for or buy any type of long-term care insurance. Thus, my best recommendation is to buy long-term care insurance and prepare your assets to prevent this from happening to you and your family.

Remember no one wants to change your diapers, so do not put this burden on your family members or loved ones. Simply buy some long-term care insurance while you are insurable and can afford it.

**Before considering long-term care insurance,
you may want to know these facts:**

• The national average median cost of one year in a private nursing home room is $74,2081. Based on the average length of stay in a nursing home of 2.8 years, a person needing care today would need more than $200,000 for a long-term care event requiring a private nursing home room. *– 1 – Genworth Financial Cost of Care Survey, conducted by CareScout, April 2009. 2 – Genworth Financial claims history*

• At least 70 percent of people over age 65 will require some long-term care services at some point; more than 40 percent will need care in a nursing home. *– U.S. Department of Health and Human Services, September 2008*

• The cost of long-term care in U.S. has increased for the sixth consecutive year. Most of these price increases are outpacing inflation. *– Genworth Financial Cost of Care Survey, conducted by CareScout, April 2009*

• There's a 68 percent probability that people age 65 and over will become disabled in at least two activities of daily living or of being cognitively impaired. *– AARP, Beyond 50: A Report to the Nation on Independent Living and Disability, 2003*

• 67 percent of people who planned to have someone help with care haven't asked; one in five caregivers said they are "not at all prepared." – *Genworth Caregiver Services Study, conducted by CareScout, August 2008*

- 6 out of 10 potential caregivers are unprepared to handle the more difficult tasks of caregiving, such as bathing, dressing and toileting. — *Attitudes and Beliefs about Caregiving in the U.S.: Findings of A National Opinion Survey, Johnson & Johnson Consumer Products Company, October 2005*

- Nearly one in five caregivers provide more than 40 hours of care per week. — *National Alliance for Caregiving and AARP. Caregiving in the U.S. Bethesda: National Alliance for Caregiving, Washington, D.C.: AARP, 2004*

- 10 percent of employed family caregivers go from full-time to part-time jobs because of their caregiving responsibilities. — *National Alliance for Caregiving and AARP, Caregiving in the U.S., 2004*

Prepare for taxes:

As I have already mentioned, taxes can be one of the biggest bites out of your retirement income, so continually knowing what is going on with the tax code can only help your bottom line. Having a tax advisor who knows and explains the changes that may affect your money is imperative. Having your taxes prepared by an actual accountant is a good idea no matter what level of expertise you may have. Let the accountant be responsible to the IRS and not you. Keeping updated about tax laws and changes as it relates to you can make big differences in your retirement dollars.

Decide where you may want to retire:

You may live in a state in which you were raised, married, worked, and have family members there to support you, but if you cannot make your retirement dollars last, then you may want to move to a more favorable state or location that does favor your retirement.

Continue to think like the rich and well-informed:

Thinking like the rich is very different than acting like the rich, and you now know what I mean after reading this book. Ways to think like the rich include: using tax strategies to your advantage, taking your time before making investment decisions, trying to make educated decisions and finding advisors who can help you make these decisions by educating you.

The next chapter is about **investor types** and how to organize all of the information and education you have read in this book and become the investor you want to become.

7

INVESTOR TYPES

Investor Types: *There are many different types of investors; some are bearish, believing that the market is going to fall, while others are bullish, believing that the market is about to rise. I truly believe you need to be somewhere in the middle. More likely, a combination of both is good practice. As a good rule of thumb, we have discussed how you may dictate the percentage of risk and safety in your plan based on your current age to prevent total loss. We have also discussed your personal risk tolerance. This section of the book will uncover how different types of investors act when investing.*

> *"Rule #1: Never lose money:*
>
> *Rule #2: Don't forget about rule #1."*
>
> — WARREN BUFFETT

Knowing what type of investor you are might help you be clearer on defining your own retirement plan.

Which type of investor are you?

You may not think that there are different types of investors, but I assure you that there are, and the ones that I have listed below are my own interpretations of client investor types from my experience as an advisor. Figuring out what traits you may have can be most helpful in planning your own specific retirement.

Not all of these investor types are so clear cut; some are a combination of others and some have their own characteristics.

Keep in mind that this is my own interpretation of investor types for illustrative purposes, so you may be able to identify your own investor type or combination of them in order to make your own unique view of investing.

Investors can be classified into the following types:

The Gambler:

These are investors who put all their money in securities, and they gamble with 100% of their principal, right or wrong, good or bad, the gambler takes chances with his or her money and can lose it all or win big.

Their percentage of assets are heavily invested in stocks and securities. They have no regard for safety and feel that the stock market will always outperform everything else. This may or may not be the case, and eventually, they get caught in a bad downturn and lose everything.

These investors feel that over time, the stock market will do best, so they might as well risk it all. However the problem is that the market as a whole may not perform best all the time. At different times buying or selling at the wrong time can be costly.

I have seen this type of investor before, and they generally do well in the beginning. But usually in the long run, they get caught in a market crash where they need money and lose substantial value at the wrong time in their lives.

This is the point at which true diversification comes into play preventing the high risk level and giving security when it is needed in the down turning markets.

My opinion is that this type of investor risks too much as compared to actual returns. You can also accomplish good returns simply by having a percentage in some safe money categories, but you do not need to risk it all. Their percentage of risk is 100 percent, and by changing this to 75/25 or 60/40 safety or somewhere in the middle they could be better diversified.

Characteristics may include:
- Aggressive by nature and sometimes over confident
- May be wealthier investors
- Can afford to take chances and losses
- Some like the action and it feels just like gambling
- May have a long term outlook on investing

The Conservative:

This investor in comparison to the gambler is the polar opposite. This investor is simply too afraid to risk anything so they only invest in bank instruments (certificates of deposits) for safety. They give up so much opportunity for growth by being so conservative. Many times this type of investor is also very frugal and they lose out because of being too conservative. Even if you show them how and they can make money safely, they still may not move for fear of losing.

This investor is too much on the conservative side, and with just a little risk they could make a tremendous difference in their bottom line.

The costs of being frugal may even hurt them when it comes to passing assets to their loved ones. Sometimes heirs are disinherited simply because they will not spend pennies to save thousands.

The conservative cannot grasp the concept that other people may know more than they do about money and how to protect it, so they lose out. By thinking more openly, they could change their returns significantly if they invested in alternative products that offer safety but keep up with inflation with market growth. They have 100 percent in safe investments, and by moving to 75/25 or 60/40 better returns now becomes more realistic.

Characteristics may include:

- Not a risk taker
- More of a saver at heart
- May seek regular steady income
- May have lost money in the market in the past
- Closed minded to new ideas

The Know-It-All:

This investor knows it all. Sometimes this type of investor cannot be educated since many of them just know more than you or anyone else does for that matter. They can cost themselves dearly by being stubborn with what they think they know.

I am not trying to insult anyone here, but it is sometimes impossible for this type of investor to learn anything new because their minds are set.

Being an expert in the financial world takes years of knowledge and expertise to understand all the products and their complexities, but this investor sometimes pretends they know everything. I cannot emphasize enough the negativity of this type of investor.

Usually they cannot be educated and are very stubborn in their beliefs even to the point that they are injurious to themselves because of their beliefs. This investor can be either 100 percent in risk or 100 percent in safe or any combination; it is their limiting belief that they know best that hurts them the most.

Characteristics may include:
- Can be aggressive or conservative by nature
- Overly confident sometimes to a fault
- May not be able to change when necessary
- May take advice from the wrong people
- Has all the answers

The Pipe Smoker:

This type of investor takes a long time making decisions and ponders things. They tend to think the world revolves around their agenda with decision making. In many ways, they are similar to a procrastinator. Sometimes they lose sight of the goal and by the time they make a decision sometimes they lose out.

To them, time is everything. The longer they dwell on something, the better they think the outcome will be. Generally, this belief is not true or sound advice with investing. Making educated decisions is sound advice, but when you cannot reach one because of your own hidden agenda it is not good. This investor can be either 100 percent in risk or 100 percent in safe or any combination; it is their limiting beliefs that they know best that hurts them the most.

Characteristics may include:
- Procrastinator by nature
- Has own hidden agenda
- Knows where they stand on an opinion
- Tends to be on the conservative side
- Sees the world through rose-colored glasses

The Believer:

These investors are too dependent on advice from their advisors, and they may not seek advice from other advisors when they should. This type of investor puts too much trust in the advice of his or her advisor. Thus, getting a second opinion is most important for the believer as you need to know if this advisor is serving you in your best interests..

Having faith and trust in your advisor is extremely important in a client-advisor relationship, but ignoring better judgment and accepting "all advice" from only one advisor can be catastrophic. Having more than one opinion on the advice you receive is imperative to the protection of your retirement. Never be too trustworthy of your advisor.

Investors should never put too much trust in any one advisor for all of their financial or investment needs, as there are too many advisors who may take advantage of that situation. These clients tend to have all of their retirement money in stock because their "broker" advised them to. Once again, there is 100 percent risk in their portfolio for no other reason other than the advisor recommended it and the client is blind to diversification.

Characteristics may include:
- Tend to be overconfident
- They tend to have only one advisor
- May only use the trusted friend for advice
- May be top-heavy with risky investments
- Has positive outlook on things even when bleak

The Perfect Investor:

This investor has it all and tries to learn as much as possible before investing or taking advice from advisors. These investors invest a certain amount in the stock market for growth, and a certain amount in safe investments for stability.

They also learn as much as they can so they can make educated decisions, the perfect investor make timely decisions in their investments selections, believe in their advisor, but also believe in second opinions when necessary. Taxes are also a substantial consideration made when investing.

If you have not already realized it, this investor type is a portion of each one of the investor types listed above. This investor type has it all without being a know it all. In contrast they are educated, knowledgeable, sensible and more importantly the perfect investor that he or she decides to be.

In being the perfect investor, you must learn that there needs to be a balance of risk and safety in their portfolio. It is crucial to know what information to ask advisors. Equally important is to know which advisor to use for which issue at hand, and never relinquishing full control of your money to any one advisor.

Remember to always consider and weigh your personal situation when considering recommendations and make sure that every situation favors yourself first. This investor type clearly understands that risk and safety need to be in balance so that loss is limited.

Characteristics may include:
- Perfectionist at heart
- Right balance for risk & safety combined
- Educates and learns on their own
- Takes time to make decisions
- Keeps emotions aside

As you can see, each of these investor types have some very unique characteristics as investors and as individuals. Sometimes their personalities get in the way and form or shape who they are as investors. I am sure there is some psychology to it. They are all different in certain ways and you as an individual investor need to find your own way in deciding what combination may be best suited for you and your retirement.

Know-it-all tips:

- Never make a check payable to anyone individually but only to the company or corporation with which you are doing business.

- Never loan money to the individual broker or advisor no matter what offer they may have.

- Be careful when your friends or family members refer an advisor to you, as you still have to check them out, and maybe even more than usual.

- Never let the trust you have for your advisor get the better of your gut feelings; if your intuition says no, then you should, also.

- Never be pressured by anyone recommending you buy right now because there will always be a tomorrow no matter what the advisor tells you.

- Be careful of family members who may have their best interests in mind instead of yours. Knowing what is best for you should always be your primary goal.

- Realize that some things are too good to be true and if they are telling you the returns are very high that means the risk level is also very high.

- Learn from the past mistakes, and try not to make them again.

- No one has a crystal ball, and no one is a know-it-all when it comes to investing money for retirement. You are ultimately responsible for your wins and losses, so do not blame anyone else.

- Getting the right advisor also means legal representation. I always tell my clients to obtain an attorney when necessary. This is important especially if you feel unable to make some of these tough decisions about your money legally.

How to protect your money:

- Use real diversification in your retirement.

- Use safe alternatives to protect a percentage of assets.

- Never give up control of your money.

- Use different advisors for different aspects of investing.

- Seek out true advisors for the specific job at hand

- Beware of the know-it-alls in life.

- Make sure your choices are best for you and not someone else.

- Slow down and take your time when considering money.

- Do not be penny-wise and pound-foolish.

- Know your own personality when investing.

- Make sure your money is always working for you.

- Never take anything for granted when dealing with advisors.

- Be careful when investing but not overly cautious.

- Always obtain second opinions on your money.

- Be open to new ideas and concepts that can help with your issue.

FINAL THOUGHTS

I enjoyed writing this book, and it was a learning process for me, as well, because it is my first book and certainly not my last. With my self-education, I found a way to make it happen — just as you can with your retirement plan.

Everyone has to seek out the right advisor for the job at hand, and a true expert can be invaluable when utilized. Knowing that costs and mistakes are inevitable, limiting these common mistakes ,and you will be substantially ahead of the game. Using the right plan can make the difference in success or failure. Also writing down a plan of action can make your success rate climb significantly. Understanding what investor type you are presently or you want to become can make your retirement journey much easier and more successful.

I truly thank you for the time you have given me in reading this book, and I look forward to helping you in the future.

Best regards,
Joseph Thomas

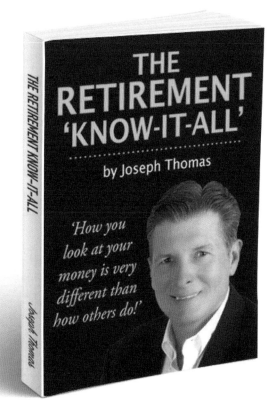